Haynes

Car Restorer's
Manual

The guide to restoration techniques

Haynes
Car Restorer's
Manual

The guide to restoration techniques

Lionel Baxter

First published in October 2003

A catalogue record for this book is available from the British Library.

ISBN 1 85960 853 1

Library of Congress catalog card no. 2003110421

Published by Haynes Publishing,
Sparkford, Yeovil, Somerset BA22 7JJ
Tel: 01963 442030 Fax: 01963 440001
Int. tel: +44 1963 442030 Int. fax: +44 1963 440001
E-mail: sales@haynes.co.uk
Web site: www.haynes.co.uk

Haynes North America Inc., 861 Lawrence Drive,
Newbury Park, California 91320, USA

Printed and bound in Great Britain by J. H. Haynes & Co. Ltd, Sparkford

Illustrations courtesy the author except where credited.

Contents

Acknowledgements

I am grateful to the following for help in providing photographic opportunities; for providing information, and for proof-reading. I am particularly grateful to **John Hardaker** for so brilliantly translating my sketches into the computerised images that form the diagrams.

Alan Denne

Chris Crookes of Classic Car Restoration Company

Paul Acred of R. J. Sutton Engineering

Dave Shiels of Halfords Super Store, Peterborough

Nick Martin of City Polishers (www.nicholas-martin.co.uk)

N and M Motors - *LPG installations* (www.nmmotors.com)

Howard Buchanan and David Giles of Leather Restorations

Burlen Fuel Systems (www.burlen.co.uk)

Tanvic Spares, Corby

Equiptech Ltd

Michelin Tyres

Mick Davison of Car Spares

Sue and Tom Duncan

Peterborough Plating Co.

Ken Freeman of AK Sportscars (www.aksportscars.com)

Geof Green

Apologies are expressed for any inadvertent use of material without permission or acknowledgement. Redress will be made in any subsequent edition or reprint of this work.

Preface

Cars have been around for over a hundred years, so the author of a book on restoring them is faced with the difficulty of where to start and where to stop. Very few of us have the privilege of owning really old cars, and in any case they would probably have been restored already, and cars that are only a few years old are unlikely to need restoration.

So, while much of what is in this book will be of general use, my target readership has been owners or restorers of cars built since the Second World War, that is, in the last 50 years or so. While engines, transmissions and electrics have remained much the same (though increasing in sophistication) over this period, the differences between cars with separate chassis and coachwork and modern monocoque construction have been noted and dealt with.

Of course, you may not be doing a complete restoration and may need information on only certain aspects of rebuilding, and I have tried to cover this, too.

The finer details of each model of car, such as tappet clearances, torque values and procedures for cylinder head tightening, etc. differ one from another, and for information on these you will need to consult the maker's handbook, the relevant Haynes manual or a one-make club technical representative. Such clubs exist for virtually every make of car and you would do well to join the one for your car. A full list of clubs and membership secretaries is available from the DVLA at Swansea, SA6 7JL (ask for form V765/1) or its regional offices. You can access this on the internet at www.dvla.gov.uk/vehicles/regoldnm.htm.

Like most enthusiasts, I spend a lot of time reading motoring publications of various sorts; consequently I have tried to make this book interesting not just for the 'hands-on' restorer but for those who prefer to dream about car restoration from the comfort of an armchair. Who knows, one day they may be motivated to pick up a spanner and feel the sense of satisfaction that comes from putting new life into an old car.

Lionel Baxter

Introduction

The creative urge most of us possess takes many forms, and if we are at all interested in cars and motoring it is likely to be channelled into spending time on improving our own vehicle or, in more extreme cases, rebuilding a complete car. On top of this, there may be other motivations for restoring a vehicle, such as wanting to own a car that we could not afford when it was new, or just to preserve something of the past. We may be attracted by its looks – something different that stands out amongst more modern machinery – by its performance, or merely 'because we always wanted one'. Almost inevitably it will be a model no longer in production.

There is the option of having a car restored professionally, but this is hardly exercising our creativity and denies us the satisfaction of acquiring the knowledge and skills necessary and enjoying the time spent practising them. In any event the high cost of professional restoration puts this route out of the reach of most of us.

At one time it was the open sports car which attracted the restorer's eye, but for some years the attitude has been that anything, if it is old, is worth saving. So all types – cars, bikes, commercial and military vehicles – are collected and restored, even those that were undistinguished in their day. The preservation movement has caught up with the motor car.

For virtually every make of car, and especially the more desirable models, there is a keen following which has resulted in the formation of one-make clubs, many of which have large memberships, some of them with their own permanent officials and extensive premises. They publish magazines, hold social meetings, have a fund of detailed knowledge of the cars they represent and often have difficult-to-obtain parts re-manufactured, which helps the spares situation enormously. If you are looking for a restoration project, and especially if you are new to the scene, it pays to join the appropriate club before you buy the car, as you will learn a lot from its magazine, will be able to contact other enthusiasts of the marque and may even be able to buy the car you are looking for through advertisements in the magazine. If you are a newcomer to restoration, a project for which spares and knowledge are easily available will save you much time and frustration, and probably money as well.

For most of us cost is an important consideration and it should be accepted at the outset that even if you undertake every possible aspect of the restoration yourself you will probably end up with an overall spend greater than the market value of the vehicle. This certainly does not deter those who are able to pay for professional restoration, who know this from the beginning (though there was a time in the late 1980s when classic cars were seen as a safe investment and so made restoration profitable), but as far as the amateur is concerned the enjoyment to be found in doing the work and the sense of satisfaction in the finished product makes it worth the cost.

CHOICE

If you already have a car for restoration you can ignore what follows; if not, there are some things to think about before you make a choice. First, beware, for few of us are likely to be entirely logical when choosing a car to restore – our good judgement being vulnerable to dreams of glamour and the promise of a bargain.

It has already been suggested that a make with a large and well organised owners' club is a good starting point. Fortunately there are many such clubs, and joining will give you instant access to a wealth of information and advice from kindred spirits. Some clubs, such as the Rolls-Royce Enthusiasts Club, run weekend technical seminars at which you can benefit from the knowledge of professional specialist restorers. If you go for a car which is obscure or one for which the production run was small, such support is unlikely to be available and you could find yourself having to spend a lot of time locating spares. You might enjoy this, of course, and there is the attraction of scarcity value and the possibility of a technically interesting job to tackle.

The use to which you intend to put your restored car is a major consideration. Is it to be for daily driving or a fun car for summer weekends? Are you looking for a sportscar for yourself or a large and impressive saloon or tourer in which you can take the whole family out? If you plan to use it frequently, then running costs (a major component of which is fuel) will probably need to be high on your agenda.

Of course, you could consider LPG. Liquid Petroleum Gas has been around for a long time and it's now being increasingly used, since not only is it about half the price of petrol, it is much less a pollutant than petrol and the number of filling stations stocking it is steadily growing. The prospect of conversion certainly widens the choice for would-be restorers. Many have been put off going for large cars because of their big engines' thirst for fuel (probably no better than 15mpg), which is a pity because it's a reasonable assumption that larger cars will have been more carefully looked after, certainly in their early years, and are much less likely to have been caned than smaller ones. (See Appendix for information on conversion.)

Garaging is an important issue. A soft-top will suffer more than a saloon if left outside in all weathers. Indeed, will you even have room for it on your drive? Insurers do not like cars that live outside (especially on the public highway), particularly in urban areas, and they load premiums accordingly. The hiring of garage space is yet another cost that you may have to factor into your calculations.

Finally, before you buy, try to get a drive in a car of similar type to see whether you will be happy with the particular model of your choice. You might find that it falls short of your expectations, especially if you don't feel comfortable behind the wheel. We are all so used to sophisticated modern machinery, that going back to an old car could prove very disappointing. By comparison they can appear extremely basic, if not downright agricultural, in handling and ride.

BUYING

Once you have made up your mind which type of car you are going to restore, the next step, before you even think of buying, is to do your homework. You cannot know too much about the make and model of your dreams. The relevant owners' club will be an important source of information, and most of the classic car magazines run articles on specific models and will supply the appropriate back numbers. From all these you can find out which are the more collectable versions, what sort of price you are likely to have to pay, the cost of commonly needed spares, the weaknesses of particular models and especially the sections that are most prone to rust.

Try to get hold of a workshop manual. Haynes publish a wide range of manuals covering many models, but if you have chosen a very old car it's possible that the book you need will be out of print. In which case, look out for a copy at the many autojumbles that take place or check your local library.

The general advice is that you should never buy the first car that you go to see. This is based on the premise that the more you see the more you will learn about the model, and you will get a feel for values. Of course, you will have to decide whether you are going for a complete re-build or just a partial one and adjust your purchase price accordingly.

When you have actually made up your mind to buy, assure yourself that the seller is the actual owner of the car. The Registration Document, V5, should indicate this provided that the seller has not assumed the identity and address given in it! If you buy from someone who is not the owner you stand to lose both the car and the cash, so check also whether there is an outstanding hire purchase agreement on it. In the UK, a call to HPI or other such organisation, will give you this information as well as whether it has ever been stolen or re-possessed. When paying, cash or a Banker's Draft are the easiest ways for both parties, and will mean that you can take instant possession of the car rather than waiting for a cheque to be cleared.

Will it be worth doing? As already mentioned, you are unlikely to cover your total expenditure if you sell the car on completion of the restoration, but to offset that is the satisfaction that restoring a car brings, the fun per hour and the knowledge that the gleaming, efficient machine which has been brought back to life is the result of your own efforts. Only you can tell whether it is worth it, but there are not many of us who do not go on to another restoration project.

SPARES AND REPAIR SERVICES

Depending on the age of your car, you may still be able to obtain spares (though they could be limited) from the local dealer, and it is worthwhile making friends with whoever staffs the parts counter as they will have access to the manufacturer's spares network and be able to look up part numbers for you on their microfiche or computer systems. If it is too old for the dealer network to carry stocks there are two other sources open to you, the factors and the owners club. Factors sell mainly to the repair trade, but they will also do business with individual customers and they carry a very wide range of spares, often going back many years. As they also sell tools and equipment they are worthwhile getting to know. The owners' club's list of spares may be restricted to otherwise unobtainable wearing parts or panels. As they are usually made in batches you may have to wait for the next lot to be made, but enterprising clubs will have bought up stock from sources that have closed down or off-loaded slow-moving items. There are also specialist suppliers who are often professional restorers themselves and who have had batches of items made up for their own use but are happy to sell them on. They advertise in the motoring magazines and have good relations with the respective clubs.

You will realise that the cost of spares is usually related to the original purchase price of the car when new, so Ford or Fiat spares are going to be a lot cheaper than Mercedes or Rolls-Royce items. However, even making allowances for this there can be unpleasant surprises as the cost of one particular component may be out of all proportion.

Remember that not every part of your car is specific to it – some parts are common to other vehicles. Wherever possible manufacturers use existing common parts to save expense, and components 'bought in', such as electrical equipment, carburettor or fuel systems and instruments, are probably used quite widely by other manufacturers. Again, the clubs are likely to know this, as will the fuel and electric specialists, and it means that availability is improved because so many units were made.

It is also not generally realised that things such as belts, bushes and bearings are unlikely to be specific to your car or its manufacturer and that your local bearing supplier (look in Yellow Pages) may be able to provide all that you require in this respect, often at a considerable saving in cost over specially sourced components. In fact, once you start asking around it is amazing what you can find and how relatively little is special to your car in the way of wearing parts.

In addition to this you will find that there are specialist services that can do almost anything you require, from making parts that are otherwise unobtainable to complete engine and gearbox rebuilds. There are back axle specialists and, of course, metal polishers, instrument rebuilders, radio repairers who can rebuild your classic radio to incorporate FM and CD input and firms that will make windscreens to any shape or curvature. In fact almost anything you may want is available from someone, provided you can pay for it.

The illustration shows a 1933 singer Sports Nine rebuilt by the author some 30 years ago. It was bought as a collection of bits and was not complete, although the collection contained seven carburettors (not all the right ones), some spare dodgy wheels, and so on. The restoration was spread out over about five years because of work commitments and the need to source parts. A fellow club member provided the seat frames as there were none in the collection of parts, and the author upholstered the seats – a first time experience – and made the trim. Restoration was, of necessity, from the chassis up; all the chrome was re-plated and the paint was sprayed with a home-made compressor. It went as well as it looked, and with its original

hydraulic brakes it was a pleasure to drive and was eventually sold to finance the next restoration.

(It was while restoring this car that I realised how common some parts were. When re-building the starter motor I visited the local electrical specialist and said, tongue in cheek, that I wanted a pair of brushes for a 1933 Lucas starter motor. The assistant leaned under the counter and produced a small box saying 'Here you are, sir, that'll be seven and sixpence.' But it's not always as easy as that!)

PLANNING

If you are going for a major restoration you'll need to do some serious planning, and this includes the financing of the project. It's likely that your costs will run into thousands of pounds, and that's on top of what you paid for the car (restorers commonly say that the purchase price is merely a down payment), and I have yet to hear of a project (including my own) that did not run over budget by a considerable margin. So, a contingency needs to be built in, especially if you are going to have to put out a lot of work to specialists.

Give thought to how long the restoration is likely to take (many take several years). Obviously, this depends to a large extent on the time you can spend on it, and perhaps also on your cash flow. Dedication to the task is the key, and you should weigh this up with other leisure interests that you may have. Then there are major changes in circumstance, such as a house move, a job change, or a new relationship – all of which can set things back for months.

Much good work can be done in the long winter evenings if your project is under cover in warm and well-lit surroundings, but if you don't have such a facility and are faced with working in adverse conditions, the lure of the local pub or an armchair in front of the TV is likely to mean that little progress is made over winter months.

A 1933 Singer Sports Nine completely rebuilt by the author.

Chapter 1

Tools and equipment

To a large extent these will depend not only on what you can afford but also on how much of the restoration you will undertake yourself. A bench and a vice, and a reasonable range of hand tools is necessary and these will include hammers, chisels, punches, hacksaws and, of course, spanners. A very wide range of these is available and you should have a set of socket spanners, a set of open-ended spanners and a set of ring spanners, or you can buy a set of combination spanners that have a ring at one end and an open end at the other. Obviously, the spanners will need to match the nuts and bolts used on your car – but what are they? The size of the bolt heads and nuts is dependent on the thread form as well as the diameter of the bolt, and for our purpose there are three types, metric, AF and BSF (which includes BSW). Metric threads will be found on Continental and Japanese cars, UNF on American and many British cars and BSF/BSW (British Standard Fine and the coarser British Standard Whitworth) on older British cars. Do not be surprised to find a mix of types on some British cars, particularly BSF and UNF.

Metric and UNF spanners are available from many outlets but you may have to look around for the BSF variety; advertisers in the magazines are the best bet.

Buy the best that you can afford. Many of the really cheap ones are of very poor quality and as you will probably never need to buy another set you might as well start with a good one, and you can do

no better than visit one of the large specialist tool or motoring stores and see what they have available.

Once you have obtained the minimum necessary you can build up your collection by buying when you need a specific tool.

Tool storage is important. It is frustrating to have to dig among a mass of tools to find the one you

Fig. 1.1. A selection of hand tools, some in sets, available from one of the larger stores.

Fig. 1.2. Tool storage. Cabinets and peg boards.

Fig. 1.3. A pillar drill and a bench grinder. The grinder is essential for sharpening tools.

it can easily encroach on working space.

You will certainly need an electric drill, both for drilling holes and for operating wire brushes and similar aids to rust and paint removal. Here it pays to buy one of reputable make and size; a minimum chuck capacity of 3/8in (10mm) is essential. Make sure also that it is of variable speed or has at least two speeds, since the single speed models run at about 1,400rpm (revolutions per minute) which is much too fast for drilling anything but small holes in steel. Make a practice of ensuring that all your electrical equipment is fitted with rubber, not plastic, plugs and sockets since plastic ones are very prone to crack when dropped on the floor or when run over.

A pillar drill is worth buying for accurate drilling of components on the bench, and these are now quite reasonably priced.

A bench grinder is also essential for sharpening tools and normally comes with a grinding wheel at both ends, one coarse and one fine. The coarse one is usually too coarse to be much good and is best replaced with a wire wheel for de-rusting components or a polishing mop. Goggles must be worn when using this tool, as small, very hot pieces of metal and abrasive powder fly off with great force and can easily damage eyes and pit spectacle lenses, to say nothing of the danger of a cracked wheel disintegrating.

need, and increasingly sets of tools are being presented in their own storage boxes. Tool boards are useful as the various items are visible at a glance and they are economical on floor space since they hang on the wall. The professionals use tool cabinets, of which there is a wide variety, so that they can take the tools to the job and store them neatly for instant access.

As far as equipment is concerned there is much available to the amateur that saves time and tends towards better quality work, but apart from the cost of the equipment it has to be housed and

JACKS AND STANDS

A trolley jack is essential for quickly and easily lifting a corner or side of a car for wheel removal or to place stands under it. A scissor jack or a bottle jack can be used instead but they're less handy. Bottle jacks can prove useful for other operations, though, such as chassis straightening.

Axle stands are essential; they do not crumble like a pile of bricks, although at a pinch blocks of wood, if of adequate size, could be used. It

Fig. 1.4. Jacks and axle stands. A small hydraulic bottle jack is on the left and a trolley jack on the right. One rated at two tonnes will be adequate for most vehicles.

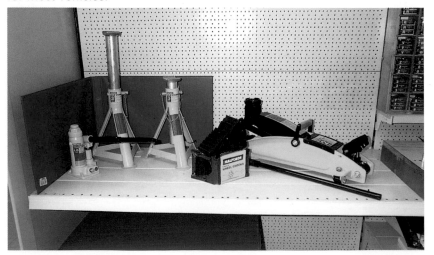

Fig. 1.5. Air compressors and tools.

should not be necessary to say that you should never get under the car when it is supported only by a jack, but people still do so, sometimes with dire consequences.

AIR COMPRESSOR

Compressed air is very useful in the workshop. Apart from clearing holes and drying components, it provides useful motive power for a wide variety of air tools, most of which are much more compact than their electrical equivalents and of course safer. If you propose to spray paint then a compressor is essential.

Air compressors come in different sizes and powers and the best advice that can be given is to buy the biggest you can afford as it will power a greater range of tools, but even the smallest is useful. The governing factor is the electricity supply; if you are restricted to 13 amps the biggest that you will be able to drive will supply about 6 cubic feet per minute (cfm) (1.7 cubic metres). This will be adequate for a reasonable range of air tools and spray painting but will not be sufficient for shot blasting.

All except the smallest compressors come with an air receiver (tank) which holds the compressed air and is topped up automatically by the compressor; one with a receiver of 25 or 50 litres capacity will do well.

Nearly all compressors will operate at pressures of up to about 100-120psi (pounds per square inch, 7-8 Bar) which is ample for all normal usage.

MIG WELDER

If you intend to repair steel bodywork yourself you will need welding equipment. The best and simplest for this purpose is the Mig welder. This welds by creating an electric arc by means of a wire automatically fed into a shield of CO_2 gas which is normally supplied from a gas 'bottle', and also acts as a filler. Small gas canisters are freely available and quite adequate, but if you are going to undertake a lot of welding using them can prove expensive and it may be better to hire a larger cylinder from one of the industrial gas suppliers (they will charge an annual rental as well as for the cost of the gas). An alternative is to buy the type of Mig welder which uses special wire with a flux built into it which creates its own arc without the addition of gas. Some welding machines can operate on both systems. A welding set capable of welding up to about 1/8in [3mm] is all that is required.

It should be noted that this is for welding steel; if you want to weld aluminium you will need a different type of gas and filler wire.

These are the essentials. If you are going to deal with woodwork you will need a bandsaw and if you get really keen and have the money – and space – there are lathes and milling machines which are very useful and can often be picked up second-hand.

In addition there are some other items which are often overlooked but which can be a real help.

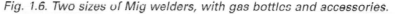

Fig. 1.6. Two sizes of Mig welders, with gas bottles and accessories.

Fig. 1.7. A high-pressure washer (right) alongside a parts washer.

Fig. 1.8. A commercial shot blasting cabinet.

HIGH-PRESSURE WASHER

A high-pressure washer, of the type for general use around the garden and for washing the car, is particularly useful to the restorer for cleaning large components and washing away road dirt, loose rust and caked-on oil and grease from the underside, especially around the suspension, before attempting to remove any of the units. If done thoroughly it makes working much cleaner and therefore more pleasant and, of course, with everything stripped bare it makes it easier to assess the condition of the various parts. If you use it in the engine bay be careful not to inject large quantities into the carburettor or breather, and wrap the alternator in a polythene bag to save washing oil away from its bearings.

WET BLASTING

Some of these washers have an accessory nozzle that allows you to blow grit and water together and you can therefore use them as grit blasters, enabling you to get rid of old paint and rust and strip to bare metal. The cleaning and preparation of parts, such as wire wheels and chassis frames, becomes much easier if done by this method, but there is a downside to it. Because of the large amount of water used, the only place to do it is outside, and the waterborne grit has a tendency to get airborne and can land in unexpected places like your neighbour's property, doing very little for your popularity. You also finish up with a large quantity of mixed grit and particles of dirt which is not always easy to dispose of. I usually dig it into the garden or 'lose' it by scattering it onto a gravel path.

As with all cleaning processes it is essential to get rid of all the cleaning agent before starting the finishing processes, and as grit collects in nooks, crannies and orifices these should be most carefully blown out with compressed air. It is most unwise to use grit anywhere near bearings or bushes that are not going to be replaced, but if you have no alternative, bearing in mind the wetness and vigour of the treatment, these items should be plugged or very thoroughly masked using waterproof materials.

Rust forms very quickly on bare metal so it should be protected as soon as possible.

Fig. 1.9. Before and after. The coil on the right has been shot-blasted and is ready for painting.

SHOT BLASTING

Shot blasting is a similar process to the one above but is done dry, using compressed air to power the grit, and as it is carried out in a cabinet or booth, is more controlled. Grit for the removal of paint and rust from steel, or glass beads for cleaning aluminium, is blown at high pressure from a 'gun' at the component placed in the cabinet. The operator puts his hands and arms into a pair of rubber sleeves to control the process and is able to see what is going on through a window in the cabinet which is illuminated.

This is a process much used in industry, but small cabinets are available for amateur use requiring only a connection to an airline and the mains electricity. The only drawback is that the system demands a hefty supply of air – a minimum of about 8cfm (1.8 cubic metres) being necessary – which is more than can be coped with by the compressors owned by most amateurs.

However, many firms offer this service and if you are undertaking a comprehensive restoration, having the components prepared in this way is money well spent as it is very effective and eliminates the worst part of the job.

PARTS WASHER

This is for parts that need degreasing, such as engine, gearbox, suspension and steering components. It consists of a small tank with a perforated shelf and a pump that gives a constant flow of cleaning fluid held in the bottom of the tank, through an adjustable nozzle. This washes away oil and

grease, aided by a good brushing of more stubborn parts which can also be left to soak in the fluid.

This is a very convenient way of getting rid of the gunge that collects on so many parts, confining the process within one compact tank which contains not only the fluid but also the filth which drops to the bottom of the tank, which you'll need to periodically pump dry and clean. All that is required is an electrical connection to operate the very low-power pump and light, if so equipped. Parts washers are comparatively inexpensive and frequently used.

IMPACT WRENCH

This is the gadget beloved of tyre fitters who use it to remove and refit wheels with alarming speed. Apart from this it has other uses. An old vehicle being restored consists of large numbers of nuts and bolts, many of them undisturbed since the day the vehicle was built and, if underneath the car, have been subject to water, salt and

consequent corrosion for many years, making them difficult to remove. If the bolt is a long one and the nut has to be unwound all the way off a rusted thread it can be difficult and time consuming. The impact wrench will usually undo very tight nuts and unwind them with ease.

I have some reservations about using the wrench for replacing and tightening screwed fasteners since there is no 'feel' for the torque. My wrench has four torque settings but the values are not given, so I use the most powerful for undoing stubborn nuts and bolts and the least to replace them, finishing by hand and using a torque wrench where necessary.

It is important when using this wrench to stick to the proper sockets that are designed for it. They are usually coloured black and do not shatter as ordinary sockets are liable to under the repeated hammering action.

An air-driven ratcheting socket driver is also useful for repetitive work and much more gentle than the impact wrench.

Fig. 1.10. A compressed air powered wrench – welcome assistance when there are 39 cylinder head holding-down nuts.

Chapter 2

Preparations

Before actually starting work on your car there are a number of things to do. The first is to prepare a place to work in, or at least to dismantle and store the various parts. When you take a car to pieces, particularly if you are taking the body off, the bits will occupy an area equivalent to about three cars, and few of us have got that amount of spare space. You will need to work first on the chassis, so that should have pride of place while the rest goes into storage – if it has to be kept outside you should prop it up off the ground using wooden battens and make sure it is well and completely covered against the elements.

Take out the seats, and if they are in good condition put them into large polythene bags. Remove all the external components such as mirrors, lights, spare wheel and find a home for them in boxes. Label them if left and right are important and also any wires that may be left without attachments. The aim at this stage should be to reduce the car to its major components, leaving each to be dealt with separately later.

Take photographs freely, and make sketches as you take things apart, especially when you get to the more detailed, intricate stuff, as after many months you will forget how it went together and it is frustrating and time-consuming to have to try to work it all out.

As far as wiring is concerned you will have to make a decision whether to try to preserve it or replace it. If it is old and rubber insulated it is likely to be perished and hardened in places – often inside the cotton-braided loom where it cannot be seen – and is best

renewed. Certainly, for trouble-free electrics, a new loom is advisable, and these are available from people such as Nottingham-based Auto Sparks (www.autosparks.co.uk) who cater for most cars. If you are a purist you can have a loom made with modern plastic-coated wires but cotton-braided like the original. Otherwise you can undo each connection and label it with masking tape and a marker or, if you are going to rewire without a loom, you can cut the wires at convenient places and either label them or rely upon the colour coding to replace them correctly.

Any pipes – petrol feed, Bijur chassis lubrication, KiGas primers, oil pressure, etc. – are likely to be in the chassis/bulkhead structure and need not be disturbed at this stage.

Nuts and bolts are best replaced in their respective holes if possible, but if not, collect each group together and put them in a marked plastic bag. It is satisfying to use new fasteners throughout when rebuilding, and many suppliers can still offer a full range including the BSF and Whitworth threads of the older (British) cars, but anything at all out of the ordinary is likely to be irreplaceable and should be kept.

Fig. 2.1. Barn find. This 1936 Standard Flying 12 is complete and restorable.

Chapter 3
Chassis and monocoque

For the purposes of restoration there are two types of car – those that have a chassis and those that do not. Originally all cars were built on a chasis frame, usually made of steel though sometimes of wood, but in the 1930s mass production brought about the development of the monocoque, or unitary construction. This meant that the frame could be dispensed with as it was possible to build sufficient strength into the body shell without it, though many cars have since used part-chassis, or subframes for convenience in mounting engines or suspension units.

The separate chassis was a long time disappearing, as late as 1955 for Rolls-Royce/Bentley, and it is still to be found on low-production cars such as Morgans, Cobras and kit cars, and Citroën 2CVs. The essential difference is that if your car has a chassis then the body can, and for a full restoration will, be removed from it to facilitate checking its alignment and to undertake any repairs necessary.

Chassis frames are usually constructed of channel section steel, the simplest consisting of two long members on either side joined together by several cross members, consequently known as a 'ladder' frame. On heavier cars and high performance models the side members were often 'boxed' by having the open side of the channel filled in and substantial cross bracing was

Fig. 3.1. A 1935 Lanchester body removed from its chassis.

Fig. 3.2. Cross-braced chassis members.

17

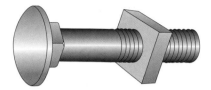

Above: Fig. 3.3. A coach bolt.

Right: Fig. 3.4. A preferred alternative to coach bolts. Ordinary bolts with substantial washers under the heads, let into sill boards for attaching body to chassis.

introduced to prevent the chassis lozenging.

There are, however, many variants. Tubular side members have been used extensively by a variety of makers, and some cars have a 'platform' chassis; in the case of the 2CV this is a simple framework covered, top and bottom, by sheet steel. There is also the Lotus type 'tuning fork' fabricated structure, and more than one maker has built cars with a single central tube of large dimensions, with outriggers.

There is also another type, called a 'space frame' which consists of a structure of small section tubes, square and/or round, welded together to form a cage-like structure on which the mechanical

components are mounted. In some cases, such as the Lotus 7 and its many derivatives, the framework is panelled to form the body.

Bodies with panelled wood frames are usually bolted to brackets on the chassis through the lower frame members; in the case of all-metal bodies, such as the Austin Healey, they may be welded. To remove the bodies of the latter the welds can be cut with an angle grinder; if the former then the coach bolts used to fasten body to chassis need to be removed. These bolts have a domed head with a squared section underneath which bites into the wood and stops the bolt from turning with the nut, but by now the nut will be rusted on and the wood rotted, so

it is unlikely that you will be able to unscrew it. They are often inaccessible, so you will have to chisel the nut off, cut through the bolt with a hacksaw blade (if you can lever a gap between chassis and wooden frame), or burn the nut off. Some of the better coachbuilders used ordinary nuts and bolts, with the heads recessed into the wooden members.

Almost all bodies of this type start at the engine bulkhead, in front of which is the bonnet. It is usual to leave the bulkhead in place on the chassis at this stage (and you may not need to disturb it all) so you will have to undo the bolts that hold the body to it as well.

Before you attempt to remove the body there are several things to do. You will probably find that there are packing pieces at the various mounting points, and these need to be noted and stored so that they can be correctly replaced when the body is put back. Open bodies have very little strength in them when removed from their chassis so it is essential to strengthen them before removal, especially across door openings, in order to maintain the correct gaps. This can be done by screwing, bolting or clamping suitable pieces of timber across the opening, or, in the case of steel bodies, tack-welding lengths of angle iron from front to rear of the opening, on the inside.

The weakest part of an open body is at the bottom of the door apertures where only the sill

Fig. 3.5. A 1939 Morgan chassis with bulkhead left in situ.

Fig. 3.6. Diagonal strengthening bars to maintain geometry while sills are replaced.

boards connect the front and rear parts. These boards are often rotten and, unless supported when the body is being removed, easily break giving you two halves of a body instead of one whole one. This is perhaps no bad thing for storage purposes but it would be better to saw the sill boards in half if rotten as you will need to use them as patterns for their replacements, and accept the fact

that you will have to spend more time later in packing the body to get the right door gaps.

Having satisfied yourself that there are no remaining connections between chassis and body you can now lift the body off backwards (to clear the bulkhead and steering) and put it away safely. Bodies, especially closed ones, are often very heavy so you will need an adequate labour

force and a well-thought-out plan of operation.

CHASSIS FRAME

You should now have a rolling chassis, and you can set about removing the major components such as engine, front and rear suspension and axles – on their subframes if any, keeping them as major units – before starting on the chassis frame.

First check the frame for its geometrical integrity (see Fig. 3.7) and make sure that the members are not buckled in the vertical plane. They should sit flat (or parallel) to the floor. On older cars without independent suspension the protrusions at the front (the dumb irons) which house the forward end of the leaf springs are vulnerable to damage. They are usually made of forged steel sections riveted to the chassis. Check that they have not been deflected downwards or sideways, and that the rivets are not loose.

Minor imperfections in chassis alignment can be rectified by the use of a jack, with a section of rolled steel joist (RSJ), or similar, and chains as shown in Fig. 3.8, but anything more major will require

Fig. 3.7. Checking chassis alignment.

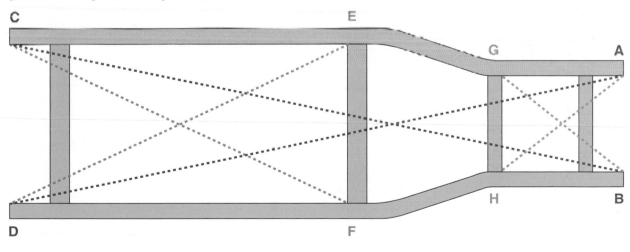

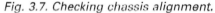

A – D	should equal	**B – C**
A – H	should equal	**B – G**
E – D	should equal	**F – C**

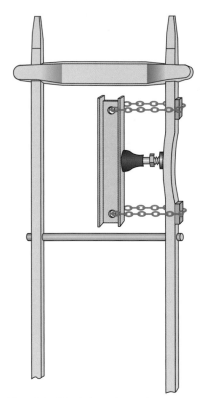

Fig. 3.8. Straightening a bent chassis member.

the section to be cut out and replaced, or you may need the help of a local body repair shop which has the necessary equipment for pushing and pulling a frame back into correct shape.

You also need to check for cracks and other damage, but first you will have to get rid of the old paint, rust and any accumulation of mud and oil. The easiest way is to

Fig. 3.9. A rotary wire brush in an angle grinder. Very useful for rust removal but eye protection and gloves must be worn.

have the chassis shot-blasted by a specialist, but beforehand be sure to protect any tapped or reamed holes as these can easily be damaged by the process. Your chassis will come back from the shot-blaster with a nice medium grey bare metal finish, which prospect may convince you that the laborious do-it-yourself-by-hand alternative – using scrapers, wire brushes and old screwdrivers – is not for you. If it doesn't, you will find that a rotary wire brush, such as the one shown in an angle grinder in Fig. 3.9, will help, but you must wear gloves and goggles to protect yourself, respectively from inadvertent contact with the revolving brush and flying debris.

By whichever method, once the chassis is clean the checking process can begin. Look for any defects, especially where there are brackets and at the suspension pick-up points. The bottom flange of a channel section frame is in tension and cracks are more likely to develop there than in the top flange.

Cars without independent front suspension were fitted with leaf springs, and to improve road-holding capabilities their chassis were usually designed to have a degree of flexibility at the front, and

this may have led to some stress fractures, and brackets, especially for the spring hangers, could have worked loose. These and cross members were often riveted on and rivets can loosen, elongating their holes. It is no good trying to tighten them by hammering them. They should be replaced with well-fitting bolts, the holes for which must first be drilled to size, or the members should be welded. Fig. 3.10 shows a strengthening plate that had to be removed to repair this area of the chassis and has been replaced with nuts and bolts in place of the original rivets. The heads have been welded over to give the appearance of rivets.

Home repairs of stress cracks or other weak areas in the frame are best done by reinforcing the frame with a section bolted in, the crack and edges being welded (see Figs. 3.11–3.15). Storage in damp conditions, such as long grass or under permanently damp coverings, can cause localised rust which may have to be cut out and replaced with new metal welded in. If a new section is required a metal fabricator can 'fold' a new piece for you and weld it in if you have doubts about your own ability in this rather crucial area.

Fig. 3.10. A new strengthening gusset bolted to chassis, but bolt heads welded over to give the appearance of original rivets.

When you are satisfied that all is well you can refinish the chassis. If you can afford it you can have it galvanised (zinc plated) which is the ultimate protection against rust, but if you do you should ensure that no further drilling or welding takes place, as this will remove the galvanising from the local area. If you have no option, then galvanising paint should be used on the now unprotected places. You'll want to put a coat of paint over the galvanising or your chassis may not look original.

Nevertheless, just paint is normally used and considered adequate. Start with a good primer, such as Ruststop, and follow with a colour coat. Traditionally 'chassis black' (available from most paint makers) is used and some brands don't require the use of a primer –

so buy the paint and follow the instructions on the tin. It's worth asking your shot-blaster (if that's the route you took) whether they offer a finishing service. You could have your chassis delivered back to you ready-painted without much strain on the budget. That way it will be protected from the start.

Depending on the type of car you are restoring and the amount of chassis that can be seen when the car is finished, you may be tempted to paint the chassis in a colour, but only do this if that's the way the original was. Usually they were black.

You should now have a perfect chassis, sitting on its stands, gleaming in its new paint, ready to accept the components you are about to rebuild.

Fig. 3.11–3.15. Repairing a chassis frame.

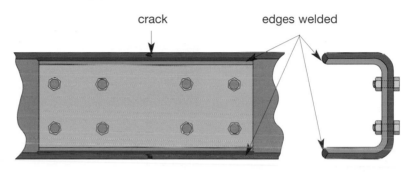

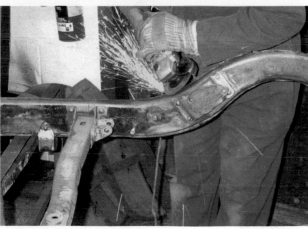

MONOCOQUES

Cars with a unitary construction body – the most common form for mass-produced post-war cars – have no chassis from which the body can be separated, but basically need the same treatment as those that have.

Strip the car of all external fittings and take out the upholstery. Wheels, suspension (complete with subframes, if any), engine and gearbox and the drivetrain should all be removed so that you finish up with a bare shell.

Professionals would remove all the glass, doors and internal trim. You may not think it necessary at this stage, but if you are going for a complete rebuild you will have to do it when you get to the body, so you might as well tackle the job now.

As with the separate chassis, you can have the body shell shot-blasted to get rid of all paint and allow inspection (and subsequent repainting) to take place. Not many firms have booths big enough to take a complete car but there are mobile units that advertise this service which is done out-of-doors at your own premises. This has drawbacks as it produces clouds of dust, shot, paint and rust particles which get blown everywhere. Your neighbours may not be too happy about this, so it's wise to construct a temporary shelter using polythene sheeting or similar on a simple frame. Incidentally, if the body shell is at all rusted (as the example in Fig. 3.16) the process can give you a nasty surprise when the full extent of corrosion is revealed. Beware that careless blasting can damage a bodyshell. In any event it will need to be thoroughly painted immediately afterwards to prevent rusting, but when you start repairs you'll have to remove the paint. So, consider whether you can deal with the repairs before you blast, and then just one paint job will do it. Or, maybe you can limit the blasting to the under pan and wheelarches

Fig. 3.16. Corroded bodywork – much more is hidden by the paint.

where repairs are most likely to be needed.

However, most of us use the more laborious way of doing it by hand, concentrating at this stage on the underside. This is rather more difficult than with a separate chassis because it is not as easy to access, so it pays to jack the structure up as high as possible unless you have an electric or hydraulic lift, or one of those much advertised pieces of equipment that either tilts or rotates the car

about its longitudinal axis making work on the underside so much easier. These are a good investment if you are carrying out a full restoration on a monocoque shell and can be obtained for a reasonable price.

Use axle stands under the body with a block of wood between them to spread the load, and before going further check the geometry of the structure. To do this use an improvised plumb line and make marks on the floor to

Fig. 3.17. Floors frequently rust through, usually from water lying on the inside.

correspond with suspension mounting points and measure these diagonally. In almost every case these should be equal, but some cars with torsion-bar rear suspension had one rear wheel slightly ahead of the other, so measure the wheelbase on each side also.

If there is a discrepancy in the measurements it is likely that the car has suffered accident damage. Careful inspection should reveal whether or not this is so. Look for welds and for crease marks which show on one side and not the other, usually at the front where most accidents take place, but possibly as a result of a side impact. Any serious discrepancy will need to be rectified by the bodyshop.

Inspect the whole of the underside for damage or rust. Some cars are prone to rusting in the floor pans, and rot in sills and jacking points is all too common. In most cars the sills under the doors form an important part of the structure and are often covered over or filled to hide the damage, so be particularly careful here.

Suspension mounting points and the areas round them must also be inspected carefully for stress cracks as well as rust, and these should be dealt with by welding or replacement by new sections.

There are specialist suppliers of panels for the repair of bodies (some for models going back many years), and repair sections are often obtainable for those areas most prone to damage or rust. Some of these sections are complex jig-built structures, and fitting them is preferable to a series of small repairs. Doing it this way will also save you time and expense. Buy the repair section (or complete panel) before cutting out the old one, as the replacement will act as a template. Fig. 3.18 shows the rot in the nose of a VW Beetle which was cut out entirely because a complete new unit (see Fig. 3.19) was available as a replacement at very reasonable cost.

Cutting out damaged panels will

depend on what equipment you have and how easy it is to gain access to it. An air-powered saw with a fine-toothed blade is a favourite of the professionals as it is small and handy in difficult places, but an electric-powered jig-saw could be used, as could a cutting-disc in an angle grinder, but it's not so precise. Spot riveting can be removed by drilling and parting with a chisel, or with a very noisy air chisel but this causes a lot of vibration and can damage delicate structures. For cutting through spot welds use a drill-mounted spot weld cutter such as a Zipcut, especially if you need to reuse one of the panels.

Fig. 3.18. A VW 'Beetle' nose rusted through.

Fig. 3.19. A complete new VW 'Beetle' nose fitted.

Fig. 3.20. Parting spot-riveted sections.

If replacements are not commercially available you will in all probability find that the one-make club which you should have joined will have had panels pressed as a service to its members, or know of a source of supply. Be careful, though, because many of these pressings are sourced as cheaply as possible and there has been much criticism of both quality and fit of some of them, especially as the thickness (gauge) of the metal is sometimes much less than the original. As a result they do not last long, and reputable restorers will have nothing to do with them.

If none is available you will have to make up the sections required or, if possible, cut out damaged areas and repair them by welding in or patching with new metal.

When this has been completed the seams should be painted with seam sealer before being finished with primer and paint. Box sections such as sills should be injected with a corrosion inhibitor such as Waxoyl or Dinitrol and the underside sprayed with an underseal.

At this point it makes sense to continue with the body of the car so that you have a structure to which the other components can be attached as each is overhauled.

Close inspection all over is necessary to determine what repair work is required. In many cases where there is rust, or bubbling paint with rust underneath it, it will be obvious, but you can never really assess the true condition with paint on, so you'll need to remove it.

If you are not going to have it blasted, then a long spell of hard work with paint stripper and a scraper will get it down to the bare metal. Paint stripper needs careful handling and is painful if you get it on the skin, so rubber gloves are essential. The procedure is a messy one as the partially dissolved paint drops onto the floor and gets wet when you neutralise the scraped area with water, or whatever the manufacturer recommends. If you are not able to do this outside it is best to spread old newspaper on the floor and take it up when dry and burn it.

When the whole body is down to bare metal you can go over it carefully and note the areas that need attention – any accident damage should be obvious. Small dents can be filled with body solder (lead filler) or resin filler, and larger ones should be tapped out from behind, if you can get behind, or pulled out with a body puller.

Panel beating is an art that takes a long time to learn. Most of us can tackle straightforward cutting and folding and bending, but three-dimensional work with compound curves needs much experience. If you are unable to obtain replacement panels or repair sections, you will need the services of a professional to make them for you.

The worst areas for rust are, not unnaturally, those that retain water and wet mud, such as the sills, door bottoms, and areas within the wings that trap mud and road dirt such as above inset headlights and within the tops of MacPherson strut turrets. The spare wheel housings in boot floors sometimes collect water when the drain holes fill with sediment, and boot lids often rust through the rear lip, simply because the manufacturer neglected to put drainage holes in it. If the car has been badly stored, especially outside with covers over it, you may find rust in the upper sections of the body and around the perimeter of the roof.

If the rot is extensive you will need to remove the doors, bonnet and boot lid and the windscreen. But, especially if the car is an open one, there is a real danger that the structure will distort, so it is essential that some form of bracing is provided, more particularly to the door apertures. Diagonal struts bolted or tack welded across the apertures will do well, but depending on the state of the body shell be generous with the bracing.

Incidentally, it is worth noting that 'solid' structures such as doors are vital in aligning panels. If you have a real 'basket case', or have bought an unfinished project, the doors will be an indispensable guide in getting the body properly sorted.

Its always a good thing to buy a donor car if you can find one and have space to store it. It can be a source of replacement panels, given that they are in a better state than the car you're restoring. Although cars tend to rust in the same places, not all have been badly stored or subject to the same neglect and you may find a shell that is, in whole or in part, better than your chosen car.

Fig. 3.21. Rust can attack upper body panels.

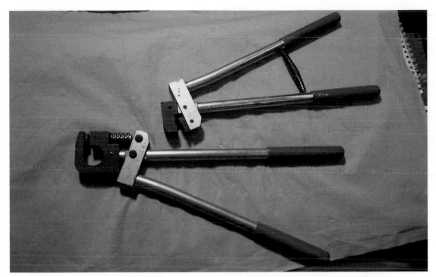

Fig. 3.22. Tools for joggling and punching holes in panels.

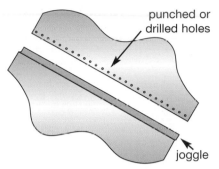

Fig. 3.23. Preparing panels for joining by joggling and welding through punched holes.

Cut out the areas affected according to the size of the replacement sections or panels and clip these in place using welding clamps, panel clamps or a few pop rivets. This is the time to make sure that everything lines up correctly and that any gaps are the same as the original – even gaps are the mark of a careful, workmanlike rebuild. When you are certain, they can be tack-welded, and then seam-welded when you are happy with the final positioning.

Where great strength is not required, such as in places where the manufacturer used spot welding rather than seam welding, it is convenient to use a similar technique. This is to punch or drill holes through one panel at intervals and weld or braze through these to the adjacent panel. This method can also be used for attaching repair sections to doors where the lower, rusted part is cut away. The replacement section is 'joggled' on its top edge using a simple tool, such as the one illustrated on the right in Fig. 3.22, and inserted behind the remaining cut panel which has been drilled or punched with a special tool (see tool on the left in Fig. 3.22). The two are then welded together through the holes and the welds are then fettled (cleaned up) with an abrasive disc in an angle grinder and the gap filled before finishing.

Complicated structures can be rebuilt by carefully copying each piece in new sheet metal and gradually building up the part, tacking it together first until you are in a position to try it for fit on the surrounding, mating structure. If you are able to make the component on the bench it is often very much easier than working on the car.

Glass reinforced plastic (GRP) replacement panels are available for many cars as a substitute for metal pressings and, although the purists may turn up their noses at them, they are a cheap and easy repair solution if your budget and facilities are limited; and they are non-rusting. You'll find advertisements for them in some of the motoring magazines.

The illustrations show an Austin A35 pick-up being restored. This is a very rare car (fewer than one thousand were made) and the owner, an A35 enthusiast, wanted it restored for preservation purposes. Whole body shot-blasting revealed it as very much a 'basket case' which called for major repair work. In order to save time and expense it was decided to cut out the windscreen pillars with the front part of the cab and the inner wing sections and replace these with parts from a 'spare' A35 saloon.

Fig. 3.24. A 'spare' Austin A35 saloon provides body panels for the pick-up.

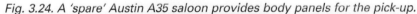

Fig. 3.25. A new section being made to replace a badly rusted area.

Fig. 3.26. The rotted out base at the rear of the cab.

Left: Fig. 3.27. Repair sections being fitted.

Below: Fig. 3.28. Panel beating tools – dollies and hammers.

The back of the cab was also badly rusted but this had to be repaired as there was no corresponding section on the saloon. The section shown being made in Fig. 3.25 is to replace a rusted area.

The rear part of the truck body needed so much repair that it was cut off from the rest of the car temporarily, as it was much easier to deal with it on its own as a smaller unit.

The base of the rear cab pillar (Fig. 3.26) and all the sections near it were rotted out and were cut away and new sections made and let in, in each case, dealing with one small area at a time so as not to lose the shape of the body. New sills were still obtainable (saving much fabrication time) and these were fitted to each side. The front part of the donor body was clamped to the inner wings to ensure that everything lined up properly before being welded (Fig. 3.27).

The body was gradually built up (Fig. 3.29). The owner had provided a pair of new front wings, discovered at an autojumble and carefully hoarded, and eventually it was possible to hang the doors and adjust them to give a good fit. They had of course been used as jigs during the rebuild. Figs. 3.30 to 3.32 show the finished body in primer ready for the paint shop.

Fig. 3.29. The body being built up.

Fig. 3.30, Fig. 3.31 and Fig. 3.32. Three angles of the finished body coated in primer ready for the paint shop.

Chapter 4

Bodywork

It's already been said that the bodywork of a chassis-based car is likely to be very flexible once removed from its underpinnings, especially if you are restoring an open car, and if you allow it to lose its rigidity it will be impossible to repair properly. Remember, therefore, the importance of bracing the body before removing it from the chassis. Bracing should be applied across the bottom of the body, across the sills and across the door apertures, preferably before the doors are removed. Any sections with major damage should be braced before removal of the offending part. Clamps are good enough for this purpose but something less obtrusive and more permanent should be used elsewhere, such as bolts or tack-welded metal strip or tubing.

Pressed steel bodies can be treated very much as monocoque structures, since they are fundamentally the same. Restoration consists in identifying faults and weaknesses in the panels and sections and repairing or replacing them, using, where possible, the same methods of joining as were used by the manufacturer unless these have proved to be unsound. Apart from detachable items like wings or mudguards, work should be restricted to the smallest practical area at any one time in order to avoid distortion.

The more traditional bodies, usually referred to as 'coachbuilt', consist of a wooden framework which is usually clad on the outside with sheet metal. On hand-built bodies this is normally aluminium in its 'half-hard' state (there are three states: 'soft', 'half-hard' and 'hard') of 16 or 18swg (standard wire gauge) thickness which is formed in various ways to the required shapes, often in small sections welded together to make complex curves, before being attached to the wooden framework by steel pins. Mass-produced cars made on this system will have pressed steel panels attached to the framing in the same way.

But not all cars were clad in metal. There was a time in the late '20s and early '30s when fabric was used with the intention of saving weight and avoiding the creaking noises that often afflicted cars panelled in metal. The fabric which has only a slight gloss, is stretched over padding that is retained on the inside by canvas. Over time, and especially if it has been painted, the fabric hardens, becomes brittle and begins to let water in. Replacement is the only answer.

The usual trouble with such bodies is that sections of the timber framing rot. Although the framing is sometimes painted it is rarely treated against rot, and water and wet mud trapped in some of the sections eventually causes damage to the wood itself which in turn can lead to corrosion in the metal. The wood used is normally ash, as this is strong and resilient, but oak is also sometimes used, especially for the sillboards and other straight members.

Fig. 4.1. Fabric-covered body on M type MG.

Fig. 4.2. Rotted body timber sections.

As is to be expected, rot usually occurs at the lower part of the body, and it is often possible to splice new wood to the old, rather than replace the whole member. But be sure to cut out all of the rotten section first.

Often the main problem is not in machining the replacement part but in gaining access to the rotten sections without damaging the panelling. Where possible, say in the case of a door or boot lid, it may be best carefully to remove the whole of the skin to give free access to what lies inside. Door skins may be held in place by their edges turned over mild steel strips that are screwed to the wooden door frame and protrude from it as in Figs. 4.4 and 4.5.

If the wooden member has rotted completely you will have problems shaping the new piece, but don't throw any of it away yet. The golden rule is to keep every scrap of wood, however rotten, until you have made the replacement piece. These horrible looking bits are all you've got as a guide, and despite their decayed state you'll be surprised how often they will yield vital information which you can use to gain some idea of the shape of the original structure, or at least enable you to take some measurements. If the part to be renewed is at all complex, and some are very complex, it makes sense to use softwood to establish the right size and shape and, once you are happy with the fit of this, to transfer the shape and dimensions to the ash that will form the finished part to be glued and screwed into position in the complete structure. This way you can make your mistakes on easily-worked cheap wood. Glue bits to it if necessary and make notes on it to help get the final part right. The good news is that modern woodworking adhesives are so strong that it's possible (and economical) to build up members of complex shape from separate

Fig. 4.3. Rotted areas cut out and replaced with new sections, glued and screwed to sound wood.

Fig. 4.4 and Fig. 4.5. Mild steel strips screwed to front and rear door uprights, protrude by about 1/2in (12mm) to enable door skin to wrap round.

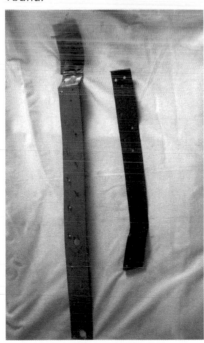

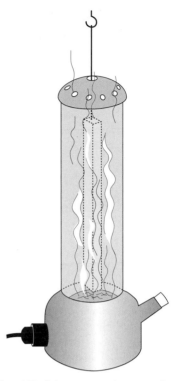

Fig. 4.7. A home-made steaming vessel for softening small timber sections, using an old electric kettle and a length of plastic drainpipe.

Fig. 4.6. New door sections made to measurements gained from piecing together bits of the old, rotted wood.

pieces of wood rather than having to hew them from single large lengths.

Laminating is another method, and it is particularly useful when having to fabricate long curved members, which if cut from large pieces of wood, apart from being uneconomical, may result in the finished item having weak spots because of the run of the grain. The process involves thin sections being layered, bent round a former, then glued together and clamped in position to hold them in place while the glue sets, after which final finishing by normal tools can take place.

There is also steaming, and you may be surprised to discover how plastic some timbers, especially ash, can be when subjected to such a process. It enables acute bends and shapes to be formed without having to worry about grain direction. The size of your steaming vessel will govern the size of timber that you can treat, of course. It's possible to build one yourself using a length of plastic drainpipe and a slightly modified old electric kettle as a steam generator (see Fig. 4.7). You will need to remove the handle of the kettle and cork up the spout, and the lid can be used to top off the drainpipe, but it must be perforated to enable the steam to escape. The piece of timber for steaming can then be suspended as indicated. Depending on the size of the timber, several hours of steaming may be required before it becomes flexible enough to bend to the required shape, after which it should be restrained round a former until it dries out. Regular topping-up of the water in the kettle is therefore necessary.

Fig. 4.8. Inside of door badly needing restoration after bodged repair.

Fig. 4.9. The front and rear ash sections, shown in Fig. 4.6, in position in door frame.

Be careful to keep all the hardware and 'furniture' that you find. Joints were sometimes reinforced with brackets or other bits of ironmongery, and the inside of doors with locks, handles, operating mechanism, window channels, etc. can be quite complex. If you need to work on two doors, resist the temptation to do so simultaneously and keep one intact as a pattern for the other; the same holds true for each side of the body, especially the wheel arches. Incidentally, where screwholes in wood have become bored out it's possible to repair them by drilling out and gluing in a section of dowel.

The sad looking mess in Fig. 4.8 is the inside of a coachbuilt door that at some time has been bodged rather than having its rotted timbers replaced. The strap hinge reinforcing the front member is particularly interesting! Fig. 4.9 shows the same door, stripped and being rebuilt. Note the new ash members front and rear and the spliced sections on the cross members.

Door hinges, particularly the bottom ones, often need attention, as a relatively small amount of wear, hardly noticeable at the leading edge, becomes greatly magnified at the trailing edge

Fig. 4.10. Wear on the hinge pin. Although apparently slight, it was enough to cause the trailing edge of the wide door to drop so much that it had to be lifted to make it close.

making the door difficult to open and close. Fig. 4.10 shows the wear that has taken place on the hinge pin. The remedy is to ream out the hole in the hinge plates and make a new pin to fit, remembering in future to lubricate it.

When putting the aluminium panelling back in place you will probably find that the lip which you had to prise up to remove it from the wood is hard and does not want to resume its original shape.

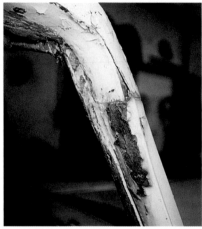

Fig. 4.11. The effect of electrolytic action between aluminium (upper) and steel (lower) parts of a windscreen pillar.

Fig. 4.12. Damaged area cut out and replaced.

In this case it needs to be softened (annealed). This is done by heating it gently with a blow torch until it reaches the right temperature. Check this by first coating the aluminium with ordinary soap – it will turn black when the right temperature is reached. The same can be achieved by periodically stroking the metal with a sliver of wood while you are heating it – when the temperature is right the wood will leave a black mark. Be careful to insulate the door's wooden framework from the heat and do not overdo the heat or the panelling will melt and you will be left with a few blobs of aluminium on the floor.

Being soft, aluminium is relatively easily dented or torn. Dents can be beaten out by the normal methods, using dollies and panel-beating hammers, annealing when necessary, and tears or other damage can be cut away and new aluminium welded in. However, this requires familiarity with the material and levels of skill which many of us do not possess, so you may have to call in professional help if the damage is extensive or complex.

The framework in some cars is based on the Italian Superleggera system, whereby steel tubing is used instead of wood for lightness. In the UK, Bristol cars were constructed on this principle. Sometimes there are corrosion problems from the dampness absorbed by the felt lagging that was used to insulate the steel framework from the aluminium panelling. If this is the case, the answer is to cut out the corroded areas and replace with sound metal, finishing by painting and insulating the two metals from each other with a plastic material which will not hold moisture.

Where steel and aluminium are in contact with each other and subject to prolonged damp electrolytic action occurs which corrodes the steel. Fig. 4.11 shows the result of this where the aluminium roof is joined to the steel windscreen pillar on a coachbuilt

MkVI Bentley, and Fig. 4.12 shows how it looked after repair.

When finished, the body can be refitted to the chassis using the same mounting system and spacers that you carefully noted when dismantling it. The bearers that lie directly on the chassis should be insulated from it; the plastic strip that bricklayers use as a damp course in building walls is ideal for this.

GRP

Glass reinforced plastic (GRP) consists of strands of glass woven into sheets (known as 'mat') of various thicknesses and textures, pieces of which are bonded together with liquid resin mixed with a hardening agent to solidify the whole. This is done in a mould and is a material much used for complete bodies on limited production cars, and has also been used for parts of bodies on mass-produced cars such as some Citroën models which at one time (on the D models) had their roofs made of it.

This is the preferred material for kit car bodies since large and complex structures can be relatively easily formed with it and, of course, it is rustproof. It is also quite strong and, although the majority of kit cars have a separate chassis, it can be used, with metal stiffening moulded in, as a monocoque. Lotus moulded the outside and inside of their Elite bodies separately and then joined them together giving great strength and good finish to both surfaces, with metal tubes for the subframe and windscreen stiffening built in.

Major damage can be repaired by cutting out the damaged area and bonding in a new section which you should be able to obtain from the manufacturer if the car is still in production, since the manufacturer will merely 'lay up' the appropriate part of the mould with GRP and so make a new section. Older bodies may be more difficult to deal with as the mould may have been broken up, in which case you can do one of two things – make a mould of your own from scratch, or make a mould from the relevant part of another car, which is where membership of the appropriate club may prove useful.

Provided enough release agent is used on the part to be moulded no damage to the 'donor' car will result. The relevant area should be treated with a suitable release agent (wax polish makes a good one), and five or six coats of this, each well polished over the area concerned, should ensure that the new GRP comes away easily without leaving any trace on the donor.

You then have your own mould from which you can make the repair section. If the area is a large one and flexible you will need to strengthen the mould by bonding in a makeshift framework to the outside, using liquid resin and glass mat. To lay up the new section, the surface of the mould will then need applications of the release agent before being treated with the gel coat. This is a coat of a thick liquid preparation mixed with the specified amount of catalyst, or hardener, which can be coloured with an appropriate pigment, if required, or it can be bought coloured. When cured, two layers of glass mat are applied to the whole of the surface, each being well stippled until saturated with resin. Particular care should be taken to remove all air bubbles and to get into any corners. A further coat of the gel mixed with resin should be applied if the repair is to the underside of the body, and especially in wheel arches, to ensure that the material is waterproof.

Leave it for 24 hours and then carefully remove it from the mould, which should not be difficult if you have been generous with the release agent.

If no original is available from which to make the mould you will have to start from scratch and try to reconstruct the shape required in wood. If it is complex you can make it in sections, the resulting

parts being bonded together later. Compound curves are difficult for most of us to form and Plaster of Paris, ordinary plaster, cement or any similar substance that can be shaped can be used, supported as necessary with chicken wire on a wooden frame. Make the best job of the surface that you can, as this is the former from which the mould is made and should be the exact shape of the finished article. The surface of this is sealed with gel, polished with release agent, and the mould taken from it.

The finish of the mould itself is critical so prepare it as well as you can, especially if the end result is going to rely on the gel coat for a finish and not be painted. You can improve the surface if necessary by finishing with wet-and-dry abrasive papers and polishing with rubbing compound. Minor hollows and imperfections can be filled with plasticene or Blu-Tack. If the part is to be painted then there is a little leeway as you can work on the surface of the finished parts to prepare them for painting in the usual way.

Cracks and minor damage can be repaired by feathering the adjacent surfaces by filing or grinding the edges and bonding them with layers of glass mat, concentrating on the underside to

give it strength. Mat comes in different weights and weaves, the heavier and coarser ones being used for the main body, so for strength this would be used on the inside of any repair, and the very fine tissue for the outside to give the smoothest finish possible.

Elderly glass fibre that has been subjected to standing water can suffer from the effects of osmosis which is readily recognised as it produces large numbers of small bubbles in the finish. If this is localised it can be cut out and replaced with new gel and mat, but if it is general the cure is to flat it off with wet-and-dry paper, bake it dry, and refinish the surface with a 'flow' coat, which is a 50:50 mix of gel and resin, after which it should be painted with polyester primer.

GRP sometimes becomes crazed, with star shaped cracks appearing on the surface. These are stress cracks caused by flexing or possibly by impact damage. This can be repaired by first strengthening the area underneath to prevent future flexing and then grinding out the damaged gel surface down to the mat. Fine tissue is then bonded on with resin which, after curing, can be finished with wet-and-dry papers, and any imperfections filled with resin filler before being painted.

Fig. 4.13. Repair of a damaged Cobra nose. The specialists were able to do this by building up mat onto metal strips first bonded to the sound GRP.

Chapter 5

Suspension

If you have an older car, particularly one with a separate chassis, it may have beam axles and laminated leaf springs at both ends. Usually there was a spring at each corner, but some cars, such as the Austin Seven, made do with three, a transverse one at the front and one at each side at the back, but Ford for many years economised with only two, both transverse, even on its larger models.

Leaf springs were fine and gave surprisingly little trouble when properly maintained, though some of the cheaper ones were prone to break and they often squeaked and groaned. The problem was that they were easy and cheap to make and few people developed them, except Rolls-Royce and a few others who took them seriously, ground their surfaces, provided them with grooves for lubrication, forged the eyes from the solid and then wrapped them in leather gaiters to keep the lubricant in and the dirt out.

Some later cars (and a good many light commercial vehicles) have a single, wide leaf, but the majority have springs with several leaves.

If your car is fitted with them the first thing to do is to take them to pieces and examine them for cracks and damage. They will be held in place on the axle by a pair of U-shaped bolts with a pair of locknuts on each leg securing a plate or bracket to the other side. This will have a hole in it to locate a pin which goes through all the leaves of the spring and clamps them together. Support the chassis and axle as you remove first the U-bolts, and then the through bolts or pins

at each eye that hold the spring to the hanger and the shackle. The spring, often quite heavy, can now be lifted away for servicing.

Remove the spring guides (clamps) and then the nut from the central pin. This is best done with the spring in the vice in case it decides to undo itself with a degree of violence. When springs break it is nearly always at the ends of the top leaf where the eye is formed, but this is not always apparent as the second leaf is also sometimes wrapped around the eye as a safety measure and takes the weight if the top leaf gives way, so this should also be checked for breakage or cracking.

Clean each leaf and check to see whether it has been indented by rubbing on the one below, usually especially obvious on the underside of the top leaf. If this is only slight

you can file or grind it out, but if it is so deep as to impair the strength of the spring you will need to have the spring remade. Usually this will entail only a new top (main) leaf as the others are cropped and re-used in their shortened form, so that the top one becomes the second, and so on, thus making the repair more economical.

If all is well, reassemble the spring on the central pin, smear each leaf with grease, such as Molyslip or Copaslip (available from Holts – www.holtsauto.com), and refit the guides. These are normally in something of a state, especially the long spacer tube on the top, but they are easily remade and must be a close fit. It should be noted that some springs are interleaved with rubber and therefore need no lubricant.

Fig. 5.1. A leaf spring guide (clamp). These are often in a poor state but can be easily made.

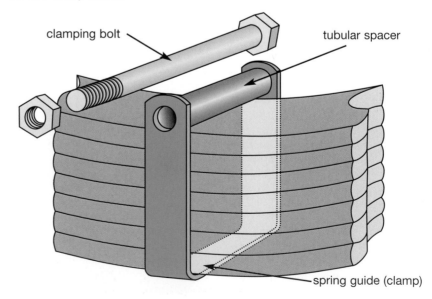

clamping bolt

tubular spacer

spring guide (clamp)

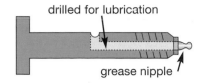

drilled for lubrication

grease nipple

Fig. 5.2. A shackle pin drilled for lubricant.

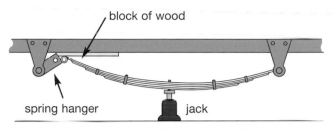

block of wood

spring hanger   jack

Fig. 5.3. Using a jack to spread a leaf spring for refitting.

You can now examine the eyes of the spring and of the shackle. On high quality cars these were forged with a bronze bush reamed for the pin and greased or lubricated from a central source, or by means of a grease nipple at the end of the pin, but the majority were of the Silentbloc variety, which consist of a steel sleeve separated by solid rubber inside another steel sleeve which is a close fit in its housing. Later versions omit the outer sleeve and the rubber itself is a press fit into the housing.

These are often in poor condition and need replacing. This is done in the usual manner by driving them out with a close-fitting drift, or pressing them out with a length of studding and a tube. Very often they will not yield to either method, leaving no option but to burn the rubber out with a gas blow torch and then saw through the outer sleeve by threading a hacksaw blade through the hole, after which the sleeve can be tapped out easily.

If it is of the solid bronze bush variety, the pin should be a close fit in the bore and not scored or marked. If it needs replacing and you do not have a lathe you will have to have some made. Be sure to drill the pin for lubrication purposes and make provision for the grease nipple.

To improve roadholding and minimize lateral movement, some manufacturers, MG and Morgan for instance, did away with the swinging shackle and ground the end of the main leaf which was housed and able to slide in phosphor-bronze trunnions. Both these and the ground end of the main leaf can wear, so they should be carefully cleaned, inspected and renewed if necessary. When

reassembling, the pin or trunnion should be lubricated with grease or Copaslip before being replaced.

Rear springs are often almost flat but front ones have a decided camber and may need spreading when refitting them in order to make the eyes coincide with their fixings on the hanger and shackle which, as a general rule, should be vertical if the spring is in good condition. If the shackle is a long way from the vertical the spring needs setting up by a specialist.

Spreading used to be done with a special tool that screwed the spring eyes outwards to lengthen the distance between them, but in the absence of this tool the spring can be replaced by first connecting the eye to the fixed shackle and jacking up the centre of the spring. A block of wood is placed between the chassis and the spring eye which slides along it as the spring is compressed until it coincides with the shackle.

Do not fully tighten the nuts on the pins at this stage if you have the rubber bush type; wait until the full weight of the car is on the springs and bounce the car up and down once or twice before final tightening with the car at its normal ride height.

As already mentioned, springs can be bound in leather gaiters, with lubrication nipples if required, but these are expensive. Tape is available which can be wrapped tightly round the spring; it is claimed that this is waterproof and holds lubrication well.

With independent front suspension you're likely to have coil springs or torsion bars, and the latter are often adjustable for ride height by increasing the tension on

them; very useful if they have settled over the years. There will be a wishbone at top or bottom, or sometimes both, to hold the upright. Often one of the wishbones will be the arms of a hydraulic shock absorber. Alternatively, especially on saloons, you may have the popular MacPherson strut suspension units, each consisting of a vertical strut enclosing a double acting shock absorber surrounded by a coil spring and pivoted between a turret at the top of the wing valance inside the bonnet and an arm at the

Fig. 5.4. A wishbone used as a suspension member – a very common arrangement. Note the transverse suspension spring.

Fig. 5.5. A MacPherson strut.

bottom constrained by an anti-roll bar which, with the arm, forms a sort of lower wishbone. Replacements for the complete unit are available. However, there's no need to dismantle the whole suspension if it appears to be working effectively.

One of the most favoured designs, now back in fashion for independent rear suspension as well as front, is the double wishbone design. This pattern often incorporates a coil-over shock absorber to provide the springing medium, though torsion bars are also quite common. Wear

takes place on the moving parts such as the pins that form the pivots and their associated bushes. If this has occurred at the front it is likely to have caused uneven tyre wear and would have given a rough and probably rattly ride if you had been able to drive the car before taking it to pieces.

To dismantle the unit it is usually necessary first to release the spring tension, but beware because springs, especially on heavier cars, can be extremely dangerous, even lethal, if they are suddenly allowed to become free. For safety's sake proper spring compressors must be used on coil springs.

To remove a coil, jack the car up and remove the wheel. Then support the lower suspension member on a jack – this will cause the spring to compress enabling you to fit a pair of spring compressors to compress it further and to restrain it. The suspension member can now be lowered leaving the spring and its compressors free for removal.

Where the shock absorber runs through the middle of the spring it must, of course, be removed first. Different designs are in use but typically they have an eye containing a bush through which a pin is inserted, connecting it to a bracket on the chassis or suspension unit, and at the other end a bolt which is secured to the body or chassis structure, with thick rubber cushions protected by shaped steel washers which sandwich the fixing point. The top of the bolt has a square or slot

which can be held to prevent it revolving while the securing nut is tightened or loosened.

With the spring removed, the state of the bushes can be ascertained by trying to move the wishbones from side to side; if there is any movement the bushes are worn and should be replaced. Undo the nuts on the bolts which pivot the wishbones to the brackets on the chassis or body structure and withdraw them and the wishbone. The bushes will have to be removed from their housings and are likely to be tight; if they are too tight to be removed by the usual methods the local garage or engineering shop will press them out for you, and the new ones in. Check the bolts before replacing them to make sure that they are in good condition and not ridged, and smear them with lubricant. If the nuts are of the self-locking variety, fit new ones and take the opportunity while the unit is dismantled to clean and paint it, and the brackets.

Torsion bar suspension usually has the bars longitudinally disposed down the length of the car (though on Beetles they are transverse), and is generally similar, with the front end of the bar splined into the lower wishbone at the pivot of the rearmost arm. With the front of the car jacked up, place a jack under the outer end of the wishbone and remove the bolt securing it to the king pin or upright, then lower the jack until the torsion bar is free of its load, at which point the inboard pivoting bolts can be removed. Mark the splined end and its housing so that it can be put back in the same place and do the same at the inner end. Also note which end is which and, if you take both bars off together, mark nearside and offside as they may not be interchangeable end-to-end and in use have become handed so are not interchangeable side-to-side. (It is worth noting that manufacturers often put stronger springs, whatever their type, on the driver's

Fig. 5.6. A telescopic shock absorber with rubber bush.

Fig. 5.7. A Jaguar double wishbone front suspension. Note absence of a coil spring as torsion bars are used.

Fig. 5.8. Spring compressors. Absolutely essential when removing coil springs.

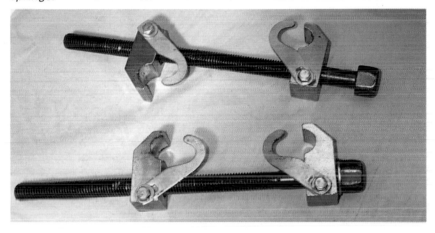

side since this normally carries a more constant weight.)

If you replace the torsion bars as marked the car will have the same ride height as before but over the years some of the tension may have gone from them and the ride height will need increasing. Some manufacturers make provision for this by pivoting the rear end of the torsion bar housing in such a way that it can be adjusted by a bolt bearing on it, while others machine a different number of splines to each end of the bar which when rotated by one spline at front or rear will increase the ride height by a predetermined amount. The

appropriate manual will give the manufacturer's settings, or your owners club will help.

The use of MacPherson struts has become increasingly common over the years, especially for the front suspension, as they can easily accommodate front wheel drive systems and have widely spaced mounting points which spread the loads nicely into the monocoque structure. Because of the height of the struts they are chiefly used on saloon cars rather than open sports cars.

As the stub axle for the road wheel is an integral part of the strut or is bolted directly to

it, the strut itself forms the upper steering pivot using some form of thrust bearing.

To remove the strut, first jack up the front of the car (under the cross member, not the suspension), remove the road wheel and compress the coil spring (preferably with a screw type compressor). The top end of the strut can be freed from under the bonnet by undoing the nut which holds it in the turret housing. Normally a single nut holds the strut in place but the strut has to be prevented from turning while this is being undone and a hexagon for a spanner is provided, or a recessed hexagon for an Allen key. In some cases the top of the strut fits into a dished housing which is itself bolted to the inside of the turret. This can be unbolted to remove the strut but will have to be removed to gain access to the bearing.

The lower end is removed by undoing the appropriate bolts securing it to the track control arm or wishbone. Depending on the design, the strut will come away on its own or complete with stub axle (and hub and brake assembly, if you have not removed these).

The various parts in the suspension system have rubber bushes as bearings. These should be examined closely for wear or deformation and replaced as necessary, as any looseness or 'slop' in the system will affect both steering and suspension and, in all probability, tyre wear. In many cases these bushes are shaped and are easy to remove.

If you wish to sharpen-up the handling of the car you may be able to replace the rubber bushes with harder, polypropylene bushes. These have less compliance than their original counterparts and offer a firmer ride with less roll and more responsive steering, although you may lose out to some extent comfort and quietness.

REAR SUSPENSION

Whereas independent front suspension has been used by

manufacturers for many years, independent rear suspension, even now, is not universal and many cars are still fitted with some form of beam axle. With front-wheel drive cars this will be an altogether lighter affair than the live axle, and may be suspended on leaf springs or coils.

The advantage of leaf springs is that they locate the rear axle both laterally and longitudinally, so need no help. Coil springs, on the other hand, are completely undisciplined and need restraining in both directions. This is usually done by means of trailing arms and/or radius rods to keep the coil upright and a Panhard rod to locate it sideways; there may also be an anti-roll bar. All of these will have rubber bushes in their joints which, like those on the front suspension, need to be checked over. If there

are signs of wear or damage they should be replaced, as apart from giving a poor and noisy ride, both handling and steering can be affected by worn bushes.

SHOCK ABSORBERS (SUSPENSION DAMPERS)

Various forms of shock absorber or suspension damper have been used over the years, both friction and hydraulic types, although you will find only the hydraulic type in more recent cars. Nevertheless, many early sports cars had the friction type fitted and spares are still available for them. The best known of these is the Andre Hertford which consists of a set of friction discs bolted together between two arms, one of which is attached, via Silentbloc bushes, to

the chassis and the other to the axle near each wheel. The amount of friction the unit affords can be adjusted by varying the tension on the central bolt, and on some better quality cars this adjustment could be made, either mechanically or hydraulically, from the driving seat whilst on the move. On larger cars, two sets would be used to cope with the weight and stress of the springs.

Removal of the central bolt on the basic type will release the discs, their brass cups and the levers, and whilst it's stripped down you can take the opportunity to clean and paint the levers. If the discs are worn or impregnated with oil or grease (which, of course, negates the friction properties on which the unit depends) they should be replaced. New discs and indicators can be

Fig. 5.9. Torsion bar suspension. The bars run backwards down the length of the car, from the lower wishbone.

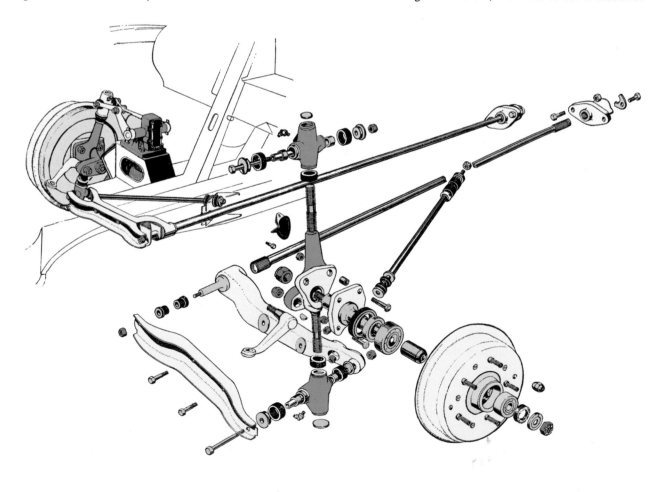

Fig. 5.10. Transverse torsion bars on the front suspension of a Beetle.

operating in cylinders filled with the appropriate hydraulic fluid. This pressurizes the fluid and attempts to push it through a small orifice. Depending on the car manufacturer's specification, these units are either single-acting or double-acting; the single ones damping only on the bump movement, and the double ones (the majority) damping on both bump and rebound strokes, being controlled by valves.

Having removed the unit, check that there has been no movement between the damper and the chassis caused by slack bolts. Dampers are in constant motion and need to be tight – elongated holes in chassis or unit are the giveaway.

Provision is made for the fluid to be topped-up periodically (8,000 to 12,000 miles). Dampers are under constant pressure and fluid tends to seep from the seals on the rocker shaft, and if this is excessive it indicates that they, and probably the bushes, need replacing, though as the cheaper ones were not bushed they will have to be replaced or sent to a specialist to be 'reclaimed'.

When the type illustrated in Figs. 5.13 and 5.14 (from a Bentley) were taken apart, cleaned and inspected, there was no perceptible wear on the

obtained from specialists, but if the arms require re-bushing you will need to send them in for professional attention. When you reinstall the units on the chassis you will need to wait until the car is finished and on the road before you can adjust them. This is a process of trial and error and you should start by tightening them up to the same moderate torque value, checking that the indicators are registering the same number, and proceed from there, altering front and rear to positions that best suit your style of driving.

The hydraulic shock absorbers which superseded the friction

dampers are of two main types, lever arm and telescopic. The lever arm type almost always doubles as an integral part of the suspension system where this is independent, their lever or levers being used to form one part of the wishbone system. Common makes were Luvax and Armstrong.

As the lever moves up and down it transmits this motion, via a rocker shaft to which it is connected, to one or two pistons

Fig. 5.12. A single arm damper/shock absorber on rear suspension.

Fig. 5.11. A friction type shock absorber.

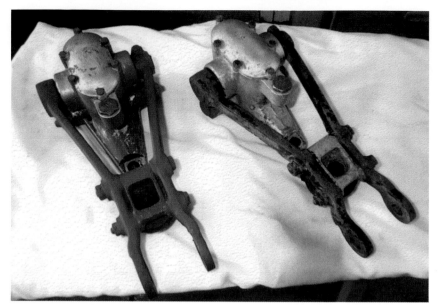

Fig. 5.13. Bentley shock absorbers forming front upper suspension members.

were replaced as a precautionary measure since the unit was already stripped. New ones were obtained off the shelf from a local bearing supplier. Although these were slightly too long, they were easily shortened on the lathe (if you don't have a lathe this can be done by careful filing). They were pressed into the body (see Fig. 5.16) then reamed (see Fig. 5.17) to remove any closing up and to ensure alignment. The supplier also provided modern, lip-type seals (Fig. 5.15 at bottom) which, since the shaft was in good condition, were a good fit and much more effective than the originals (Fig. 5.18).

The rocker-shaft splines had been marked to ensure that the rocker went back in its original position – important because if not correctly centred the pistons could collide with the casing when approaching the end of their travel. The pistons were replaced and the unit built up (Fig. 5.19).

As with all hydraulic devices, it is necessary to be very careful

pistons and cylinder bores but the fluid level had shrunk to the bottom of the rocker shaft, indicating leakage, even (in this case) when not in use. The seals were the original type of square section rubber (Fig. 5.15 at top) which were extracted simply by hooking them out with a small screwdriver. The bushes showed slight signs of wear and

Fig. 5.14. Bentley unit stripped and cleaned.

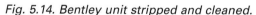
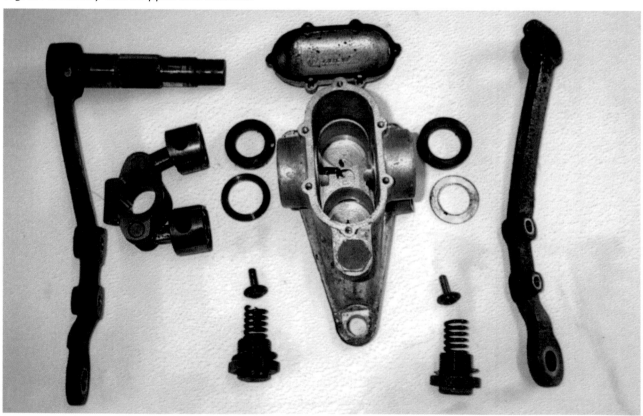

Fig. 5.15. Old and new seals for the Bentley hydraulic damper.

Fig. 5.16. The new bushes being pressed into the body of the damper unit.

about cleanliness to ensure that no foreign bodies, however minute, are present in the system and that there is nothing to contaminate the fluid, which on this type of shock absorber is in fact ordinary SAE20 type lubricating oil, but normally a special hydraulic fluid is required.

As mentioned above, if you don't fancy rebuilding your own units, or if they are seized or too far gone, there are specialists who can rebuild them for you or supply replacements. Take care that you use a reputable firm as many so-called reconditioned units have had little more attention than a change of oil and a lick of paint. It's probably better to get new units to be on the safe side.

At the more recent end of the range you'll find that most cars are fitted with telescopic hydraulic shock absorbers, the vast majority of which are, like so much else, non-repairable throwaway items. Examine them carefully to see whether they have been leaking, check the rubbers at both ends for damage, and test them by pushing and pulling them open and closed. A steady resistance should be felt. If there isn't any at all, or if it is erratic, replacement is the only answer for most of them. However, a few types – especially the adjustable version of Koni – can be rebuilt by the manufacturers and should be returned to them or their agents.

Fig. 5.17. Reaming the new bushes.

Fig. 5.18. Replacing the seals. The new ones, of a modern pattern, as shown in Fig. 5.15.

Fig. 5.19. The pistons being replaced in the body.

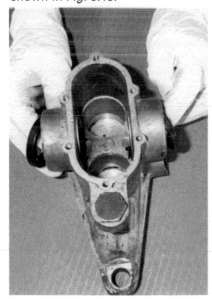

Chapter 6

Steering

If there is play in the steering it must be removed, or at least minimized. Such play may be caused by wear in any one or more of the many joints in the system, and the nature of steering geometry is such that even small amounts of play in these joints will be magnified at the steering wheel.

With the wheels on the ground, have someone gently move the steering wheel from side to side while you check how much play, if any, there is in the linkage. If any exists, try to identify, by watching the movement of the various parts, at which joint or joints the movement is lost. Then, with the front jacked clear of the ground, grasp each front wheel in turn at front and rear and see if there is any movement which does not revolve the steering wheel. Next, grasping the wheel at top and bottom, attempt to rock the wheel; if there is movement here, then wear exists in the king pins or swivel joints and this must be eradicated first.

Older cars with beam axles, and some later models with independent

suspension, have the stub axles (or uprights) held to the axle or suspension unit by means of a short shaft – the king pin (see Fig. 6.1). This is attached to the suspension, and the stub axle which pivots on it is fitted with bronze bushes which wear with use and/or lack of lubrication, and need replacing.

The way king pins are secured varies from model to model, but quite often it is a cotter pin which can be removed by unscrewing its retaining nut and tapping the pin out. After this, on some models, the king pin itself can be tapped out with a drift, having first removed any grease retaining caps at top and bottom, and taking care to retrieve the thrust washer, but many of them have an internal screw thread for extraction purposes. If this is the case, screw an appropriate length of studding into the pin, put a long sleeve (made from a tube of suitable diameter) over it, run a washer and nut down the studding to rest on the sleeve and turn the nut to draw out the pin. The bushes can then be tapped or drawn out in a similar way and replaced with new ones,

ensuring that any holes for grease nipples line up and that the thrust washers underneath the axle, on which the weight of the car is taken, are properly assembled and greased. The new bushes should be reamed as they may have become distorted.

On cars with independent front suspension the system may have ball-joint swivels. The bearings or swivels must be renewed to take up all wear, and the steering joints themselves can then be checked.

The track rod which links the two front wheels and transmits steering motion to them, or the tie rods in the case of rack-and-pinion steering, terminates in track rod ends. These perform two functions; they link the steering arms to the rest of the steering system and they provide adjustment for the effective length of the track rod. The track rod ends (see Fig. 6.2) consist of a short arm with a taper for fitting to the steering arm and a ball joint in the screwed housing. These are now throwaway items, but on older cars could be dismantled and taken up for wear. The ball is spring loaded, and in good condition should have no 'slop' but rather a slight resistance to movement. If it is too free, or its dustcover is torn, it should be replaced. Note that track rod ends are handed with left- and right-handed threads to suit those on the track rod itself.

These can be detached by unscrewing the retaining nuts and withdrawing the tapered arm. They are usually very tight, and a special tool (readily available) can be used to part them by means of screw

Fig. 6.1. Kin pin and bushes.

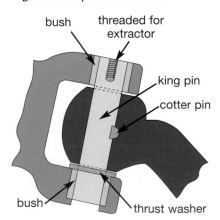

bush

threaded for extractor

king pin

cotter pin

bush

thrust washer

Fig. 6.2. Track rod end.

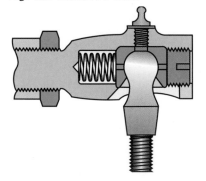

Fig. 6.3. Exchange rack and pinion steering unit.

pressure or a forked wedge driven between them. Provided you can get a good swing at them with a hammer an easy way is to place a solid object in contact with the steering arm and give the opposite side a sharp blow with a heavy hammer.

Before unscrewing the lock nuts on the track rod or tie rod, count the number of exposed threads so that the replacement can be returned to the correct position, otherwise the tracking will be affected.

If the car has independent front suspension and a steering box instead of a rack-and-pinion system there will be more joints in the system and some rocking shafts with bearings, each of which must be in good condition and without play, so check each one all the way back to the drag link/drop arm junction at the steering box.

Rack and pinion steering systems, first introduced on a large-scale production car by Citroën in 1936, have gradually almost completely taken over from other systems and are simple and trouble free, but can of course wear with use or lack of lubricant. The lubricant on the majority of cars is grease or a specified quantity of oil, sealed into the unit, though provision for routine lubrication is included on many of the older versions.

If there is no play in the rack, check that its mountings are secure. These are usually clamped and sit in rubber pads which sometimes are found to have suffered from leaking oil and become squidgy and therefore in need of replacement. Tighten them to the torque value specified in the manual. Also check the condition of the expanding gaiters that are clamped to the rack at one end and the tie rod at the other as these contain the lubricant, and if torn or punctured are an MoT test failure.

Most racks have no adjustment points (on some earlier ones there was a spring-loaded adjustment for the pinion) and are not repairable; but they can be exchanged.

It you do need to replace the rack, or want to alter the steering ratio to get a more direct feel for the steering and reduce the number of turns of the wheel from lock to lock, you may be able to obtain a quick rack with a different ratio.

Steering ratios are model dependent. A heavy car (without power assistance) will probably have a ratio of say 4:1 (or even more on an American car) which means that four complete turns of the steering wheel are necessary from one lock to the other. On a smaller, lighter car the ratio may be 3.5:1, and on a sports car 3:1, which

gives sharp, direct steering (but not as direct as the 1920s GN which had a cable and bobbin steering system with a ratio of 0.5:1, or its successor the Chain Gang Frazer Nash with a ratio of 0.75:1).

Earlier cars and some 4x4 vehicles are fitted with steering boxes rather than rack-and-pinion systems. A variety of different types have been used and wear can often be traced to them. It should be noted, though, that even when new most had a few degrees of free play at the wheel, especially on full lock, and none was as precise as a rack-and-pinion system. Although the MoT tester may allow up to about 3in of play, when overhauling the system the aim should be minimal backlash – try at least to get it to less than 1in on a 14in steering wheel. Before the introduction of the test some systems were allowed to deteriorate so much that anything up to about 180° was not unknown, with drivers progressively compensating for the gradual increase in sloppiness!

First check with the wheels on the ground, or otherwise locked, that the mounting of the box is secure. Flexing of mounting points is a possibility on chassis mounted boxes, and if there's evidence of this the box should be reinforced so that no movement takes place.

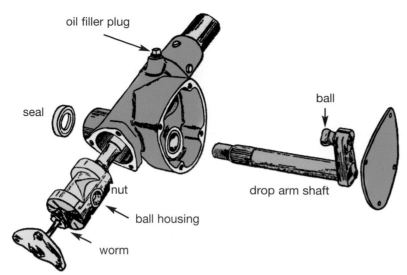

Fig. 6.4. A Burman-Douglas steering box. The bronze 'nut' can wear and is replaceable.

Some of the most common types of steering box are as follows:

BURMAN-DOUGLAS

This is a worm and nut steering gear (see Fig. 6.4). A phosphor-bronze nut, which is a close fit in its housing, slides up and down on a coarse thread, or worm, turned on the end of the steering column, and transmits this motion to the drop arm by means of a ball on the end of a short lever that engages in the nut. Wear takes place on the thread of the bronze nut, which is replaceable and still available from specialists. If the new one is tight, place it in a vice, suitably packed so as not to damage its surface, and

screw the worm up and down, lubricating it well with paraffin.

Wear can also take place in the bushes for the drop arm shaft and these should be replaced.

WORM AND NUT

This is similar in construction to the Burman-Douglas described above, but has provision for adjusting the travel of the lever and therefore the steering lock. There is no adjustment for wear, and reconditioning is as above.

CAM AND LEVER

This is not dissimilar to the worm and nut, but omits the nut. A peg on the end of a rocker shaft engages the worm direct and moves up and down the worm threads when the steering wheel is turned. The rocker shaft can be adjusted so that the peg engages the worm more deeply; a bolt on the top of the cover is provided for this purpose. See Fig. 6.5.

WORM AND WHEEL

A worm on the end of the steering column engages with a worm wheel which is mounted directly onto the drop arm shaft. Wear takes place on the wheel and can be rectified by unbolting it from its mounting on the drop arm shaft, or if keyed to it, cutting a new keyway, and rotating it by a quarter of a turn to an unused part of the wheel. Some types also have a bolt on the end of the column which can be screwed up to reduce end play in the worm. There is also adjustment for the end thrust of the drop arm shaft, the bearings of which should be inspected for wear.

WORM AND SECTOR

This is a variant on the above but has only a segment of a wheel instead of a complete one. Some of these have an adjustment whereby the sector is meshed more closely with the worm but if this does not take up the play it

Fig. 6.5. Cam and lever steering box. The peg can be made to mesh more deeply with the worm by means of the thrust bolt on the top cover, and end play of the shaft can be taken up by removing shims from the end cover.

Fig. 6.6. Worm and sector steering box.

cannot be revolved like a complete wheel, and so building up the teeth and re-cutting, or replacement, is the only solution if badly worn.

MARLES STEERING GEAR

This is one of the best (see Fig. 6.7). The worm, which in the highest quality systems is mounted on roller thrust bearings top and bottom, is hour-glass shaped to coincide with the arc described by the rocker arm with which it engages by means of a roller. The roller itself is mounted on ball races onto the rocker arm by means of a pin which is eccentric and can be unlocked and turned to mesh the roller more or less deeply with the worm.

End play of the worm is taken up by screwing the steering column more deeply into the steering box, a clamp on the box itself being slackened to allow this.

RACK AND PINION

Early versions of this system could be adjusted by screwing the adjusting screw inwards to make the rack engage the pinion more closely. Most modern systems are not adjustable but quite cheap to replace or have rebuilt.

In each case check that there is no up and down play in the steering column itself. The bearing at the top of the column is sometimes made of compressed felt which is fundamentally

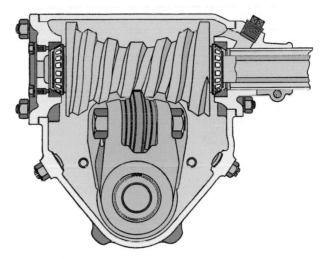

Fig. 6.7. Marles steering gear.

unsatisfactory and should be replaced if at all possible. See whether you can replace it with a ball race or at least a bronze bush. Some columns are shimmed at the steering box cover and can be adjusted by the removal of one or more of these, and some by a bolt that takes the end thrust.

Lubrication of the steering box is usually by means of oil rather than grease since this flows to all parts of the mechanism, but it is not unknown for owners to make up a mix of thick oil and grease to try to take up play in a worm box, and one well-known maker of lubricants offers a compound said to achieve

Fig. 6.8. Rack and pinion steering.

this. All too often old steering boxes are not oil tight, their oil seals being either inadequate or worn, so attention should be paid to this when overhauling them.

The geometry of steering and the suspension of front wheels is complex and governed by angles that affect the amount that the wheels toe in or out (they are seldom parallel), and their camber and castor. Camber, the way the wheel leans in or out when viewed from the front, is often not adjustable and is more concerned with suspension than steering. Castor angles, the amount by which the wheels trail behind the actual

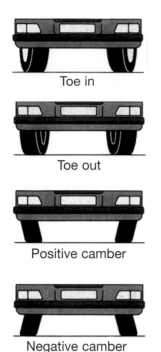

Toe in

Toe out

Positive camber

Negative camber

Fig. 6.9. Toe and camber of front wheels. (Michelin)

steering centre, are sometimes adjustable but are best left alone unless the steering is very heavy, in which case the angle can be reduced slightly. The amount of toe is important and is the reason why track rods and tie rods are adjustable at their ends. In general, the average car, especially if driven by the rear wheels, has the front wheels toeing in at the front so that the measurement between the front of the wheels is slightly less than between the back of the wheels, usually by about 1/8in (3mm). This is because forward movement of the car tends to open them out. On a front-wheel-drive car there is a tendency for the wheels to toe in when driven so it is usual to set them to toe out slightly.

The best way to have these measured is at a tyre specialist, all of whom have the necessary measuring equipment. However, you can set them up yourself reasonably accurately by centring the steering wheel and placing two straight edges, packed to the same height, in contact with the outsides of the front wheels, and taking measurements immediately in front of and behind the tyres. Adjustment of one piece track rods is made by slackening off the track-rod-end lock nuts and turning the rod so that it reduces or increases its effective length. Some rods have a hexagon formed on them for this purpose; if not you will have to use a pipe wrench or Mole grip on the tube itself.

Tie rods on rack and pinion steering must be equal in length when set, so that it is necessary to count the number of exposed threads at each end and make sure that these are the same. Finally, check that the steering wheel itself is centred – if not you will have to continue your adjustments.

POWER STEERING

Many more modern cars are fitted with power assisted steering, made necessary by the increased weight of engines and their ancillaries and the wider tyres used as a consequence.

Power steering systems have a hydraulic pump connected to the engine by a belt, which therefore runs continuously once the engine is started, the fluid being pumped to the return side of the reservoir when not needed, sometimes through a cooler. As the wheel is turned a valve at the bottom end of the column opens, pressurizing the appropriate side of the steering gear, closing when movement of the column stops.

The steering gear and pump are generally not repairable so replacement will be necessary if the system fails, but first check that the driving belt to the pump is in good condition, and then that the system is filled with fluid. Replace and re-tension the belt if at fault and if the system lacks fluid, re-fill. If it has been sucking air you will need to bleed it. One way of doing this is to fill the reservoir and, with the wheels off the ground, move the steering wheel slowly from side to side to help the system to fill, topping up as necessary. Then crank the engine over in short bursts (remove the wire from the ignition coil to prevent the engine starting), still turning the steering from side to side and topping up the reservoir. If the fluid looks discoloured it will be caused by tiny air bubbles – wait a few minutes for these to disperse before completing the job. Test drive and check the reservoir once more. Any leaks will mean replacement of the appropriate component or seal, and reference to the manual will give details of the appropriate procedures and torque values.

On earlier cars steering columns consist of rigid tubes enclosing the shaft which actuates the mechanism, and as it is often very conspicuous it pays to make sure that it is well finished. However, for many years now columns have consisted of an open shaft with universal joints. These are necessary to enable the shaft to get round any obstructions and also, sometimes aided by other devices, to ensure that it collapses under frontal impact. The universal joints can wear and need to be checked, as does the bearing at the top (steering wheel) end.

Some cars have a bearing that consists of compressed felt; this is best removed and a plain bush or ball race substituted. Be careful, however, because sometimes there is a felt bush intended to hold lubricant, in addition to something more durable.

Steering wheels come in an amazing variety and range of sizes. These are generally suitable for sports cars and may look odd in a saloon, so you may need to keep the original. The wheels on older cars were often finished in a black plastic material, or celluloid on even older ones, and these can be re-finished in a nylon substance, but may respond to treatment with a plastic polishing compound as covered in the section on workshop practice. There are specialists who provide a reconditioning service, and some wheels respond well to powder-coating.

Chapter 7

Hubs

It is essential, especially on the steered wheels, that the bearings on which the hubs run are in good condition. Had you driven the car before starting the restoration process and detected a rumbling sound, the bearings would be the prime suspects. It is easy to test them to find out for sure. With the wheel jacked up and squarely in front of you, grasp it firmly at opposite sides and push and pull in order to detect any evidence of free play.

Remember that any play in the horizontal plane may be caused by wear in the steering system, especially the track-rod ends, and in the vertical plane by the steering swivels, but if you get play in both planes check the wheel bearings anyway.

To get at the bearings you need to remove the outer part of the hub. If the car is fitted with drum brakes, the drums are usually secured to

the hub by means of two or three countersunk screws and may be removed either with or without the hub, although on some models drum and hub are integrally cast and cannot be separated. If there are disc brakes, the calliper should be undone and supported clear of the disc but not left hanging on its hose; tie it up out of the way. Remove the hub by first taking off the hub cap which is almost always a push fit in the hub and can be prized out with a screwdriver in the flange provided, tapping the screwdriver lightly if necessary – hammer blows directly on to the hub cap itself will only damage it.

The hub will probably be retained on the axle by a castellated nut, usually prevented from revolving by a split pin or shaped cover with a projection fitting into a slot on the axle. On some cars the nut is 'handed' so that in the unlikely event of the nut revolving when the car is

Fig. 7.1. A hub cap – keeps grease in and grit out.

in motion it tightens up rather than loosening itself. If they are 'handed' those on the off side of the car will have a normal right-hand thread, while those on the near side will have a left-hand thread. (Such cars will have their wheel nuts similarly handed.) There is no doubt about the Bentley hub in Fig. 7.3.

The hub bearings are normally a press fit in the hub and a push fit on the axle, so the hub can simply

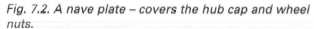

Fig. 7.2. A nave plate – covers the hub cap and wheel nuts.

Fig. 7.3. A Bentley hub. No doubt about which side this goes.

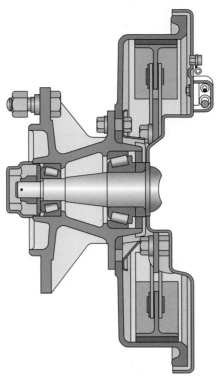

Fig. 7.4. A typical front hub with drum brake.

be pulled off though occasionally a hub puller may be necessary.

Bearings have for many years been of the taper roller type, but earlier cars had deep-race ball bearings that took the thrust as well as the radial loads; the taper roller type do both and are usually more compact. The inner races and rollers (usually caged) come away easily, leaving the outers in the hub. They should not need removing unless you intend to replace them, when they can normally be tapped out with an old screwdriver or drift (but check first that the race is not held in place by a circlip). The larger, inner race will then free the oil seal which sits inboard of it. In some cases bearings are separated by means of a tubular distance piece which will also come free.

The greasy mess should be cleaned out and the races inspected for signs of wear and pitting; grease in the brake drum or outside the hub will tell you the state of the seal, which is always worth replacing. In cases where the inner race cannot be tapped out, a special knife-edge bearing puller will be required.

Repair kits are usually available for more modern vehicles and include all the necessary replacement parts; otherwise you will have to source them separately.

When refitting or fitting new bearings you can either press the outer races into position or tap them in carefully, preferably using a short piece of tube, the diameter of which should be close to that of the outer diameter of the race itself. If this is not available, use a brass drift and gently tap them equally in at least three different places around their circumferences, a little at a time, until they are firmly seated in their housings, not forgetting to include the spacer if provided. Do the same with the seal – open side inwards – and if it is an old-fashioned felt ring, try to replace this with a modern type of lip seal.

Pack the appropriate grease into the bearings – if in doubt, use a light molybdenum disulphide grease – and an additional small quantity either between the bearings or in the cap. This acts as a reservoir; if the hub overheats the surplus grease melts and runs into the bearings but if you overdo it the grease will be forced through the seal and onto the friction surface of the brake drum or disc.

Reassemble, not forgetting the spacing ring at the rear (if there is one) which goes on first, and any washers under the nut. With drum brakes, if the drum is detachable, replace the hub without it so that the brake shoes cannot bind, and adjust the nut until the hub will not revolve (this will ensure that the bearings are seated correctly). Then slacken off until the hub rotates freely with barely perceptible end-play. With the non-detachable type of drum, ensure that the brake shoes are slackened off to the fullest extent. If you have a handbook or manual it may give a measurement for the amount of end-play required.

Lock the nut with whatever device is provided and replace the cap, tapping it in gently to secure it. Replace the brake mechanism and give the hub a final spin to ensure that nothing is binding with the drum or calliper in position.

Hubs on front-wheel-drive cars are generally similar, but instead of fitting on to a stub axle they slide onto the splines on the end of the constant velocity joint that provides the drive to the wheel. The retaining nut is probably secured by means of staking the reduced portion on the outside with a punch into the groove on the end of the shaft (Fig. 7.5).

Fig. 7.5. Staking a retaining nut.

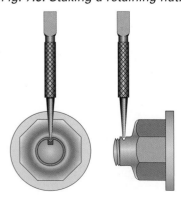

Chapter 8

Wheels and tyres

As the car's only contact with the road surface it is essential that wheels and tyres are in good condition and of suitable type. It is many years since wooden artillery wheels were replaced by pressed-steel wheels, and these remain the norm, though wire wheels tended to be favoured for sports cars. More recently there has been an increasing use of alloy wheels.

Pressed-steel wheels rarely give trouble, but because kerbing and driving over rough terrain may have damaged the rim edges they should be inspected carefully and revolved on one of the front hubs to check for truth and concentricity – If there is more than 1/16in (1.5mm) run-out, the wheel should be discarded, or, in the case of wire wheels, trued.

For do-it-yourself repairs of minor damage it pays to first remove the paint – this is where shot blasting comes into its own, especially if the wheels are wire-spoked. Examine carefully for cracks. These can be welded if not too severe. Check around the rim and between any holes, and fettle well any welds for the sake of good balance. Pitting can be filled in with weld unless it is very deep or extensive. However, most wheels are so readily available at breakers' yards that replacements could be the easier option, unless yours are so special that you want to keep them for the sake of originality.

Wire wheels look the part, but they can be troublesome and difficult to clean, and they often emit creaking noises. They are also heavier than pressed steel wheels and appreciably heavier than alloys

of equivalent size, as well as being less rigid. They also need respoking after a number of years, but there are plenty of specialists able to do this and fit new rims if necessary. Spoked wheels obviously have to be fitted with inner-tubes, and one of your checks should be to see that none of the spoke ends stand proud of the top of the spoke nipple. File or grind them down if any do, because if they are not flush they may puncture the inner-tube. Similarly, the rubber liner that fits over the rim and prevents abrasion of the inner tube must be in good condition.

Wire wheels may be bolted to the hub or, more likely, be fitted with a knock-off nut with two or three 'ears', or a hexagon for a special spanner. The drive to the wheels is by splines; the hub is splined externally and the wheel hub internally and it is important to ensure that the splines are clean, lightly greased and in good condition. If the car has run with a wheel nut not properly tightened, and the wheel consequently not fully locked on and seated to the back of the taper, the splines may have become damaged. Known bodges in such circumstances include the use of foil or very thin shimming material in an effort to restore grip. If you find that this has happened, your options are either replacement or getting the splines re-cut by a specialist.

Some wheels, wires and pressed-steel, are driven by pegs in the hubs instead of splines, and in this case it is necessary to ensure that the holes have not been

elongated through movement between the hub and the wheel. If the pegs do not fit well in the wheels the holes will need welding up and re-drilling.

Tension in wire wheel spokes should be equal. You can judge this by tapping them and comparing the musical note that they emit. Any loose ones should be tightened or replaced, being careful to maintain the truth and concentricity of the rim. This is probably not a job you should tackle yourself, though, as it calls for great skill and proper equipment. For safety's sake it's better to go to the professionals.

Alloy wheels are lighter than pressed-steel or wire wheels so, if you wanted to (for extra grip on the road, for instance), you could fit larger diameter wheels given that there's enough room under the wings to allow the suspension to bottom out without the wheels hitting the wheel arches. Alloys are more fragile than the other types and consequently more easily damaged by kerbing, and they are subject to corrosion, particularly from road salt in places where the protective lacquer coating has been chipped off. Also, with age, they tend to become porous and there may be a deterioration in air-tightness around the tyres resulting in pressures not being retained for very long. The cure for this may be coating the inside of the rim with lacquer, but an inner tube usually provides the most satisfactory solution.

The outside of the wheel is normally protected by clear lacquer which needs removing with a paint

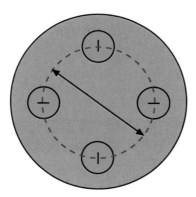

Fig. 8.1. Pitch circle diameter (PCD) – or how far apart are the wheel studs?

remover such as Nitromors or similar, when it can be tested and examined as detailed above. If in good condition you can re-polish them and paint any areas that were so treated originally, finishing with a coat of clear lacquer.

Check the wheel nut holes and ensure that you have the right type of nuts for the wheels. Some wheels have steel sleeves inserted in the holes, and some have nuts with extended sleeves that fit in the holes. Wheel nuts, new, are often quite expensive and can cost as much as a set of second-hand wheels, but the correct type are essential for safety.

Many people are tempted to fit wheels of a larger width than were originally fitted by the manufacturer, especially when changing to alloys. This gives greater adhesion, of course, and may look better than the perhaps rather skinny wheels/tyres they replace, but if you overdo it you may lose out on the feel of the steering – and very wide wheels often look silly and can do nothing for the ride and handling of the car. If you are making a change of wheels, bear in mind that the stud pattern and pitch circle diameter must be the same as on your hubs, and the offset must also be the same or you may have problems not only with steering but with clearance under the wing.

TYRES

Earlier cars ran on crossply tyres; radial ply tyres came in, courtesy of Michelin, in the 1950s and did much to transform grip and ride, to say nothing of the life of the tyre. If your car was originally fitted with crossplies you can change to radials but on some cars you will lose some feel and character and it's wise to talk to someone knowledgeable in the owners club before doing so. If you do change, the law says that you cannot mix tyres on the same axle; they must both be radial or crossply. You can have different tyres on different axles but it is best to run on the same type front and rear all round.

Tyres are extremely difficult to design and there are many different sorts for different purposes, but each is marked with information about its intended purpose, size and speed rating (see Fig. 8.3).

It goes without saying that tyres must be in good condition and kept properly inflated, and if the car is laid up for any length of time remove the wheels from the car and store them out of direct sunlight. If you are not able to do this, at least cover them and jack the car up to relieve them of their weight.

Fig. 8.2. Offset and outset of wheels.

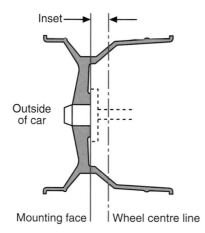

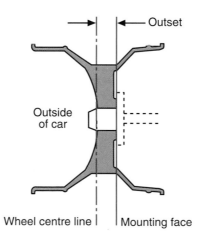

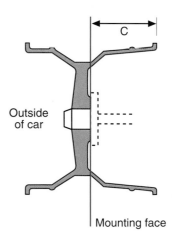

Inset is calculated by measuring in from the hub face to the wheel centre line.

Outset is calculated by measuring out from the hub face to the wheel centre line.

The 'C' dimension is the measurement from the wheel mounting face to the edge of the inside rim.

1. Denotes type of construction.
2. Speed symbol.
3. Uniform tyre quality grading markings required by USA consumer information regulations (not required in the UK).
4. Manufacturer's name or brand name.
5. North American tyre identification number.
6. Tyre size designation, (old form) incorporating speed symbol (S).
7. Denotes type of construction (radial).
8. M&S (mud and snow) marking where applicable indicating that the tyre has a winter type tread pattern.
9. Reinforced marking where applicable.
10. A commercial name or identity.
11. Load Pressure requirement. (not required in the UK).
12. Location of tread wear indicators (markings not on all tyres).
13. Tyre size designation. New ECE form followed by load index and speed symbol.
14. Load index.
15. The word tubeless where applicable.
16. Country of manufacture.
17. North America Department of Transportation compliance symbol.
18. ECE type approval and number.
19. Tyre construction details (not required in the UK).

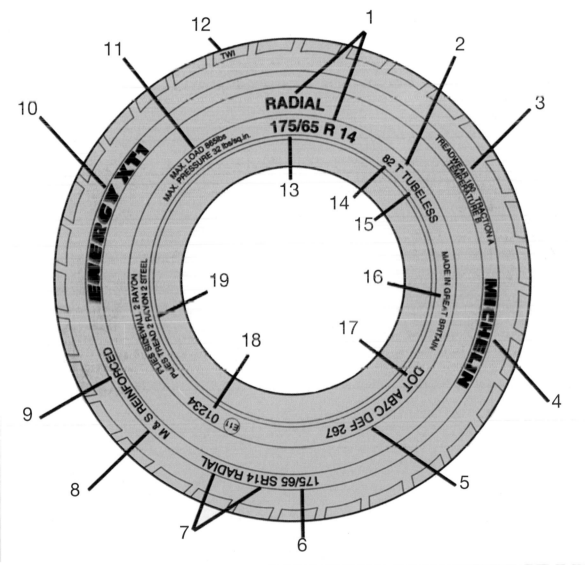

Fig. 8.3. The writing on the tyres – what it all means. (Michelin)

Chapter 9

Brakes

Depending on its age, your car's brakes will be either drum or disc, or a mixture of both – discs at the front where most of the work is done and drums at the rear. At low speed drum brakes are more effective than discs, and they are particularly good as handbrakes – which is not always true of discs, witness the D series Citroën. Also dependent upon age, will be the system by which your car's brakes are operated. Even though hydraulics began appearing as far back as the mid-1920s, many manufacturers continued to use cable and rod operated systems for a long time after that, and Rolls-Royces and Bentleys had a mix of hydraulics and rods up to the mid-1950s.

If you are unfortunate enough to have a car fitted with one of the Bendix mechanically actuated systems, you are strongly advised to convert to hydraulics. There were many different types and all are complicated to adjust and difficult to keep in good working order. Other rod and cable systems when well maintained and properly adjusted in the first place can be effective, but before considering the method of operation we will start at the actual brakes themselves since they all operate on the same general principles.

DRUM BRAKES

On older cars brake shoes were pivoted at top or bottom and opened out by means of a double-sided cam which was partially rotated by pressure on the brake pedal (or handbrake lever). This

system gave way to an expander type made by Girling in which the shoes are forced apart by means of a conical wedge which, when the brake pedal is pressed, is pulled between two rollers thereby forcing out two plungers which then bear on the brake shoes bringing them into contact with the inside of the brake drum. The expander unit is able to slide, or 'float' slightly on the backplate to allow the brake shoes to centralise themselves in the drums when operated – all the braking stresses being taken by the adjuster. Most of the work is done by the leading shoe (the one to the left of the expander when the drum is in normal rotation), and improvements were made to spread the load, including the addition of a strut to the other, or trailing, shoe, to move the toe of the shoe (at the adjuster end) outwards, thus converting the unit to two-leading-shoe operation. With hydraulically-operated systems the shoes are worked by means of wheel cylinders from which two plungers expand outwards when the brake pedal is pressed.

Before attempting to remove the brake drum, slacken off the shoes. Drums are usually held in place by countersunk screws which are often chewed up and may need careful work to free them – if all else fails, drill the head off using a drill about half the diameter of the head. If the drum is stubborn and will not draw off, first ensure that the shoes are fully retracted, and if this does not help, tap it on the front with a soft-faced hammer. If

you hammer it on the side you may distort it, and if it has cooling fins you will damage these. Some quality cars have two threaded holes in which bolts are screwed to draw the drum off, while others have integral hubs and brake drums so that it is necessary to remove the hub to take off the drum.

Although any replacement shoes that may have been fitted would probably be asbestos-free, cars older than about 15 years originally had asbestos in the friction linings, so it is a sensible precaution to remove any dust carefully and avoid inhaling it, just in case. Don't blow it out with an airline – try the opposite, a vacuum cleaner. There are available aerosol cans of a preparation that can be sprayed onto brake shoes and drums which will clean off the harmful asbestos dust.

As with all mechanisms, when first dismantling note carefully how everything goes together and sketch or photograph it before disturbing anything, for although the principles are the same, there are many variations of detail.

Inspect the inside of the brake drum. The working surface should be bright and smooth. If it is at all pitted, as a result of rust, or is scored, which happens when a foreign body gets lodged onto the friction surface of the linings (or worse, has run directly on the face of the shoe as the lining has been completely worn down at some stage) then the drum will have to be machined to restore an acceptable surface. This is done by grinding or skimming in a lathe, an

Fig. 9.1. Removing scoring in a brake drum by turning in a lathe. A trued mandrel is essential.

inexpensive job that any machinist should be able to do for you. Alternatively, if you have a big enough lathe of your own you could do it yourself, but you will first have to turn up a mandrel to fit snugly in the register that fits onto the hub, as you cannot assume that anything else is truly circular. Some drums have their maximum diameter stamped or cast on the flange and should not be reduced beyond this value. If in doubt consult the manual, or the owners club. If the car has been standing for a long time with the brakes on, the drum may be

distorted and will 'grab' when the brakes are applied, and so should be tested for truth with a dial test indicator.

If you are not sure, find some better ones, but if yours are rare they can be reconditioned with new steel liners or you can have new ones made by a specialist.

Drums should be cleaned and painted on the outside; a VHT (very high temperature) paint such as is used for manifolds looks good, especially in colour if they can be seen behind wire or alloy wheels, but traditionalists will want to keep to black or silver.

Next, strip the backplates. There's a special tool for removing and replacing brake shoes, but an adjustable spanner will do just as well. If there are small steady springs (see Fig. 9.8) fitted through the web of the shoe, free them – usually by pushing in and twisting the retaining washer and then pulling out the pin from the rear – and any other linkage. With the adjustable spanner fitted to the top of one of the shoes, ease it gently outwards and towards you until it is free of the expander unit. The top of the other shoe can now be freed by hand and the upper spring released. The shoes can then be eased away from the adjuster unit or abutment and lifted clear. The pull-off springs are probably of different lengths and values and if you are planning to reuse them you'll need to mark them so that they can be correctly replaced. The best policy is to renew them, though, as it's quite likely they'll have stretched.

For many years now friction linings have been bonded to brake shoes and they will need to go to a specialist for replacement. If you have rod or cable operation, ask for soft linings to be fitted. For mass-produced cars you can probably buy replacement shoes over the counter. If you have linings that are riveted to the shoes, the soft copper rivets can be cut flush with the back of the shoe with a pair of side-cutting pliers and then knocked out with a punch, and the new ones riveted into place, starting at the middle and working towards each end. Linings are brittle and need careful handling.

Fig. 9.2. A Girling adjuster unit.

Fig. 9.3. A Girling expander unit showing working parts.

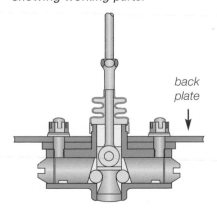

Fig. 9.4. A Girling adjuster unit showing working parts.

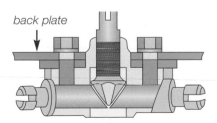

Fig. 9.5. A backplate being prepared for painting.

brake shoe

lining

Fig. 9.6. A snail cam bearing on inside of shoe.

Support the head of the rivet with a rod of about the same diameter as the rivet head in a vice and tap a punch into the hollow shank of the rivet to expand and secure it.

The expander mechanism can now be taken apart, but if you remove it completely be careful to note the exact position of the actuating rod. The two plungers are prevented from falling out of the housing by means of pins. Remove the pins and extract the plungers, being careful not to lose the rollers. They should be a smooth sliding fit but will often be found to have seized if unused for a long period, as will the expander cone itself, in which case it is easier to remove the unit and work on it at

the bench. The cone can only be extracted one way; remove it and clean all the parts thoroughly before inspecting them. The cone, rollers and plungers are hardened and seem to wear well, but renew as necessary and rebuild with a smear of white brake grease on all the moving parts and replace the gaiter if necessary.

The adjuster unit on the Girling type brake is a single unit and, unlike the expander unit, is firmly bolted to the backplate. It also has two plungers held apart by a cone with flats machined on it. Pull the plungers out and screw the cone up until it comes free. Again, clean and grease everything before reassembling and unscrew the cone until it is clear of the plungers.

If the backplate itself is damaged, it should be restored

before painting and reassembly, which is the reverse of the process described above, bolting the adjusting unit tight and leaving the expander unit slightly loose. Lay out the shoes and link them with the spring at the adjuster end and fit into their slots in the plungers, having first smeared a little white grease onto them (and at the expander end). Put one shoe into the expander, fit the spring and then gently lever the other shoe outwards so that it too drops into its slot.

Replace the drum and tighten the adjuster cone until the brake is hard on, then screw the nuts holding the expander unit, with their double coil spring washers underneath them,

Fig. 9.7. Snail cam adjusters on hydraulic wheel cylinders.

Fig. 9.8. Alternative types of steady spring.

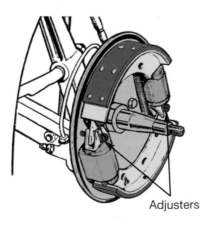

Adjusters

until they are tight, after which they should be slackened off one complete turn and new split pins used to lock them. The adjuster is then slackened until the drum is just free to revolve without contacting the shoes.

The method of anchoring the brake shoes, and adjusting them, may differ, especially with hydraulic systems. The most common methods of adjustment are by means of snail cams or screwed expanders. On some types of snail cam the shoes rest in contact with the cam, and adjustment is made by turning the cam with a spanner on the squared end of the cam pivot protruding through to the rear of the backplate. On front brakes each shoe is normally separately adjusted so there are two squared ends, whereas rear brakes usually have one. The squared ends of adjusters often have their corners worn away through spanners of the wrong size having been used. The assembly is normally riveted together making repair difficult, so if they are too far gone you may have to replace the backplate complete. In any case, while the brake is stripped, ensure that the cams are free to turn.

Another type of snail cam adjuster is a small unit that fits between the expander unit plunger – usually the piston of a hydraulic wheel cylinder – and the shoe itself and is operated by turning it with a screwdriver. Two holes are provided in the drum for this purpose, but again it is common to find only one adjuster for the rear brakes.

Screw adjusters are a part of either the shoe anchorage or the expander unit and alter the distance between the two shoe ends. This is usually done by means of a serrated wheel with a spring bearing on it to prevent it rotating of its own accord. Access is via a slot in the backplate and when the wheel is turned (using a small lever or screwdriver) it produces an audible click. The slot should be covered by a rubber plug

to prevent water and road dirt getting in.

If the car is really old – '20s or early '30s – it may have cam operated shoes, in which case the cam spindle and bush should be inspected for wear and be replaced if necessary. If you have had to remove much metal from the drums in the process of skimming them, the shoes will no longer be concentric with the drum. If adjustment for lining wear is by means of an adjuster on the heels of the shoes this does not matter as it will be compensated for when adjusting the brakes, but if not you should, if possible, pack the shoes out at the cam or expander unit until they are concentric with the drum.

Some drum brakes have a self-adjusting mechanism which works by expanding with the shoes when the brake pedal is operated, and allowing them to retract only sufficiently to give clearance. There's a variety of types and each one's method of working can usually be established by inspection. It is important when rebuilding the brake that the mechanism is returned to its zero position otherwise you may have difficulty in refitting the drum.

RODS AND CABLES

Although eventually eclipsed by hydraulics, mechanically actuated braking systems in good condition are perfectly satisfactory if properly adjusted and maintained. The basic requirements are that there should be no slack in the various joints and that they should be adequately lubricated. The majority rely on forked rod ends and clevis pins which, of course, wear – the pins becoming waisted and the rod end holes elongated.

New pins of various sizes and lengths are still available from motor accessory shops, and if you can't replace the rod ends, the elongated holes can be drilled and reamed oversize; or if too far gone, welded or brazed up and then redrilled. As they all suffer lack of

lubrication and the worst of conditions underneath the car, smear the moving parts with a molybdenum disulphide grease, Copaslip or something similar.

Mechanical braking systems are set up at the factory and should not need adjustment, but in the nature of things cars that have passed through several hands over many years may have had the system tinkered with. Apart from servicing or renewing the connections as suggested above, and re-bushing any sleeved components such as equalisers, no adjustments should be made to the rods themselves unless they are damaged or it's obvious that they have been interfered with. One sure sign of this is that the levers and compensators do not lie in the right positions. At rest, and with the brake shoes properly adjusted, they should lie behind their dead centres so that pressure on the pedal moves them in an arc towards the dead centre, maximising the travel and leverage. Get rid of all lost motion in the system, which should be under very slight tension, and seek help from the owners club.

Cables should have as easy a run as possible and their conduits should have grease nipples. New cables, with a wide range of fittings, can be made up by specialists. Handbrakes still rely on mechanical systems and often appear as something of an afterthought, in many cases having exposed cables running round pulleys or guides. Here again, while the system is stripped, the application of a generous helping of long-lasting grease is advisable.

DISC BRAKES

Disc surfaces should be smooth and without deep grooves. If yours are grooved it's possible you could have them ground – many have their minimum thickness stamped onto the edge of the disc but reference to the workshop manual will give you this information if not otherwise available.

Fig. 9.9. A brake disc. The marking on the edge reads: 'MIN TH 8mm'.

The method of securing the calliper to the suspension varies from model to model. In general they are bolted through the calliper body with two bolts. Remove the calliper and then the pads from their securing devices – often long pins, but springs are not uncommon. If the pads are in good enough condition to re-use, put identification marks on them so that you can refit them correctly. Before undoing the flexible hose, either put a clamp on it to prevent the hydraulic fluid escaping or place a small piece of polythene sheet over the mouth of the reservoir and then screw the cap back on. The hose can then be disconnected and the calliper removed to the bench for cleaning and inspection. The most common arrangement is that of a piston bearing on the brake pad on either side of the disc ('fixed' calliper) being forced inward under hydraulic pressure, though some have a single piston ('sliding' calliper).

The open end of the piston which bears on the pad often becomes rusted especially if its dustcover has been damaged – pistons and cylinders must be bright and shiny and without any marks of rubbing or scoring.

Pull off the dust cover and take out the piston. This may be easier said than done as they are often very reluctant to move. Try gentle levering on the dustcover seating groove, but take care as the metal is thin and you might break it. If this is not successful, try blowing it out with an airline in the hole where the flexible hose goes, but mind your fingers and place a flat piece of wood in the calliper opposite the piston as it often comes out with considerable force. If this fails, connect it up again to its hose and pump the pedal hard, bearing in mind that hydraulic fluid will be blown out as well as the piston. If this also fails, try blanking off the hose connection and use a grease gun to force grease through the bleed hole, but be careful to remove all traces of the grease with white spirit before rebuilding the unit.

Inspect the piston and cylinder and clean them thoroughly. As with all hydraulic components, absolute cleanliness is essential. If they are in good condition, rebuild the unit using a repair kit which will include a new seal and dustcover.

Smear the cylinder walls and piston liberally with hydraulic fluid, fit the seal using fingers only, since tools are likely to cause damage (and are unnecessary anyway). A special grease should be supplied in the repair kit which is smeared onto the piston behind the groove. As you carefully insert the piston, press the dustcover into position in its groove.

Ensure that the piston(s) is/are fully retracted, then replace the calliper and tighten the bolts to the torque specified in the manual. The pads can now be fitted and secured and the flexible hose reconnected. Do not forget to remove the clamp or the piece of

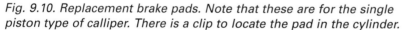

Fig. 9.10. Replacement brake pads. Note that these are for the single piston type of calliper. There is a clip to locate the pad in the cylinder.

polythene sheet from the reservoir before attempting to bleed the braking system.

HYDRAULIC SYSTEMS

The main advantage of hydraulic brakes is that they are simpler and maintenance free – no lubrication of joints or connections, no stretching and, especially, no problems with compensation since, pressure being equal, the same amount is applied to each wheel. The components are a master cylinder, actuated by the foot pedal, a system of rigid and flexible pipes and the wheel cylinders at each wheel. Connections in older cars may be from the master cylinder to all four wheel cylinders, but more modern vehicles will have split or dual circuits. These are so connected that normally all wheels are braked together but in the event of problems with one circuit, reduced braking is still available by means of the other.

Most later cars of any size or performance will have a brake servo, using vacuum from the intake system (or a separate pump on diesel engines) to assist the pressure applied by the driver, and many have brake apportioning valves which vary the pressure in the rear brakes to prevent their locking-up under light load.

On pre-war cars original brake piping would probably have been made of copper, but on later standard classics it's more likely to be of steel, and if your car is fitted with steel pipes you must replace them as they notoriously corrode from within. The replacement tube of preference is Kunifer tubing (a cupro-nickel alloy). If you are going to make up your own pipes you will, of course, need a flaring tool (these can be bought at reasonable prices) to prepare the ends of the pipes to fit the unions. Alternatively any good accessory shop will make them up for you. There will be two flexible hoses at the front, and either one at the rear

Fig. 9.11. A single-circuit type of master cylinder with piston and pushrod assemblies removed.

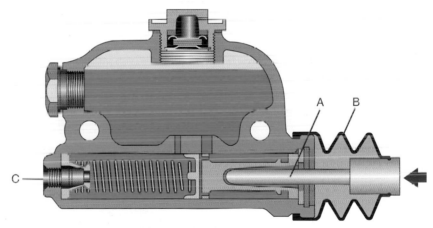

Fig. 9.12. A single circuit master cylinder.

Fig. 9.13. A twin-circuit master cylinder – note divided reservoir.

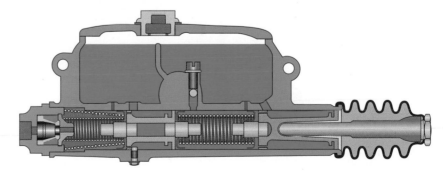

Fig. 9.14. Female (left) and male (right) flared ends on hydraulic brake pipes.

in the case of a live or beam axle, or two if independently sprung.

If the pipes on your car are already of Kunifer tubing, carefully check for cracking or deterioration and replace any suspect sections. Also ensure that they are adequately clipped to the chassis or body frame.

Repair kits are available for master cylinders and wheel cylinders and include all the parts to rebuild these units. However, some are sealed units. (The wheel cylinders are best rebuilt while the rest of the brake is being serviced or overhauled but are dealt with here for convenience).

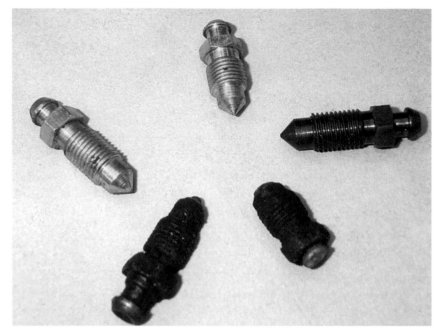

Fig. 9.15. Bleed screws. The one at lower right has suffered and was difficult to remove.

WHEEL CYLINDERS

If you are rebuilding the braking system completely there is no point in conserving the fluid so get rid of this by undoing the connection to the wheel cylinder and pumping the brake pedal until no more fluid flows from the pipe or hose. You will not be re-using the fluid so dispose of it thoughtfully. Undo the bolts

Fig. 9.16. The various parts of a typical wheel cylinder.

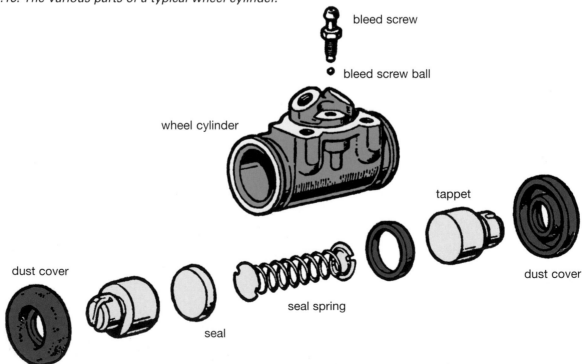

bleed screw

bleed screw ball

wheel cylinder

tappet

dust cover

dust cover

seal spring

seal

holding the cylinder(s) to the backplate and remove it to the bench. The cylinder is dismantled by removing the dustcovers from the cylinder and sliding the piston(s) out, followed by the seals and the spring. Clean the cylinder and pistons, using methylated spirits, examine the bore which should be unmarked (if it is marked the complete assembly should be replaced) and check the condition of the bleed screws. These are often rusted in and have the spanner-flats on their hexagons rounded through abuse from ill-fitting spanners (make a resolution to buy a proper brake spanner). In cases where you cannot get a grip with a spanner, put the bleedscrew in the vice and undo it by turning the cylinder. New bleed screws are available from accessory shops.

With everything clean and dry, lubricate the cylinder bore with new hydraulic fluid and reassemble the unit. If you are not replacing it immediately and there is a tendency for the spring to push the pistons out, put a rubber band around them to hold them in place.

THE MASTER CYLINDER

The master cylinder is usually connected directly to the brake pedal, but on some cars, normally intended to have left-hand-drive, they may be on the nearside of the car and operated by a torque tube from the pedal. The reservoir for the hydraulic fluid may be integral with the master cylinder or remote from it and connected by a pipe. On earlier cars it will be a metal container, but more modern cars will have a translucent plastic container. Similarly, if there is a brake servo this may be integral with the master cylinder, in which case it acts directly on it, or it may be separate from it, in which case it acts on the wheel cylinders. Earlier, inexpensive cars will have a simple master cylinder with only one outlet, whereas others will have two, either on the side of the cylinder or one at the side and one at the end, since they are in fact two separate units in one cylinder.

Remove the connections to the cylinder, the cylinder itself and then the connection to the pedal – on some cars this is merely a push rod into the piston.

There are numerous designs of master cylinders, but the majority are dismantled by removing a circlip at the pedal end of the cylinder after the plastic dustcover has been removed. The piston and valve assemblies can be carefully withdrawn and kept in the same relative positions on the bench, while a note is made of them.

After cleaning the cylinder, inspect the bore for damage. Hydraulic fluid is hygroscopic, that is it tends to absorb moisture, and if it has not been changed very often, and especially if the car has been standing for any length of time, globules of water can collect and start rust formation. This usually happens on the lower surface of the cylinder and, of course, scoring can take place if impurities have been present in the system. If this is superficial you may be able to lap out the cylinder using fine emery or wet-and-dry paper wound round a piece of dowel wetted with light oil, and operated by an electric drill on slow speed. If you do this, move it backwards and forwards the full length of the cylinder to keep the bore parallel rather than concentrating on one or more parts where the rust may have pitted the surface. If the damage is at all deep and you cannot easily get rid of it by this method you will have to either replace it with a new one or a better second-hand one, or, if replacement is expensive or not possible, find a specialist who will bore it out and reline it with stainless steel to match the original bore size.

Rebuild the unit with the repair kit and lubricate with new hydraulic fluid. If you are not intending to use it immediately, blank off the various apertures to prevent the ingress of moisture and dirt.

While the master cylinder is out of the car, check the brake pedal itself and its bearings. If it is relatively modern it will be hinged at the top (unless it is a VW Beetle) and is likely to have a nylon bush which is replaceable if worn. Older cars may have bottom hinged pedals, supported by a short shaft together with the clutch. These will be bushed with bronze and may have some provision for lubrication (which is often neglected because of the awkward position): if there is any slop the bush should be renewed and light grease applied.

SERVOS

Except on diesel-powered vehicles, which have a vacuum pump, and certain Rolls-Royces and Bentleys, which have a servo driven by the gearbox, hydraulic systems make use of the vacuum present in the inlet manifold (this can supply a force of about 30psi to lighten the amount of pressure required to slow or stop the vehicle). Although servos have been fitted for many years on larger cars they have come into their own where disc brakes are fitted, as these require higher pedal pressures than drum brakes, so they will be found on all but the smaller, lighter cars.

As mentioned above, servos operate either directly on the master cylinder and are attached to it, or, if separate, on the hydraulic system itself. If the car is in working order you can test the servo while stationary by pressing the brake pedal several times to exhaust the vacuum, then, while keeping the pedal depressed, start the engine and you will feel a quite noticeable 'give' in the pedal. With the engine turned off, after a short wait, an audible hissing noise will be made by the servo if the pedal is again depressed.

Carefully examine the pipe connecting the unit to the manifold as any puncture will cause leakage and stop the system working. Also check the non-return valve fitted into the pipe at its junction with the manifold to ensure that this is working satisfactorily.

Many modern servos can't be serviced and need to be replaced if faulty, but some older ones can be dismantled and repaired. Reference to the handbook will guide you, but the surest test is whether you can obtain a repair kit. If you can, it will contain instructions about fitting, but first make sure by cleaning and inspection that the large unit housing the diaphragm has not been punctured, because if it has it will not operate and a replacement will be your only option.

PRESSURE LIMITING VALVES

Many cars are fitted with pressure limiting valves, the purpose of which is to prevent the rear wheels locking up when the rear of the vehicle is lightly loaded. There are various patterns, some of which are linked to the rear axle, the deflection of which controls the pressure in the hydraulic lines to the rear brakes, while in others pressure to the rear brakes is either cut off entirely or limited to a certain value. These are not normally repairable (again, check whether service repair kits are available). If a replacement is fitted of the variable pressure type it will need adjusting when it is in position, the measurements and procedure being given in the relevant manual.

BRAKE BLEEDING

Air, unlike liquid, is compressible, so for the brakes to operate efficiently there must be no air in the system. If present the result will be erratic, unbalanced braking. It is therefore necessary to bleed the brakes after working on the system to get rid of the air. Fill the reservoir with new, clean fluid, being careful not to spill any on paintwork as it is

Fig. 9.17. A brake bleeding kit. The tube incorporates a non-return valve.

an efficient paint stripper. If you get any on yourself wash it off immediately as it is poisonous. Starting at the wheel furthest away from the master cylinder, get someone to pump the brake pedal while you loosen the bleed valve at the wheel by about half a turn. The valve should have a plastic or rubber tube attached, the other end being placed in a clean glass jar. As it is pumped out the hydraulic fluid will at first contain air bubbles, but eventually it will come out as a solid stream of fluid. Your helper (who should ensure that the reservoir does not run dry) should be asked to pump slowly and hold the pedal down at the end of each stroke. When all air is expelled the valve can be tightened and the next wheel dealt with. When all four have been done, after a few strokes the brake pedal should feel solid after the first inch or so of its travel. If not, the procedure should be repeated.

There are various gadgets on the market to make this operation possible for one person. The cheapest is merely a tube with a non-return valve fitted (see Fig. 9.17) so that pumping of the pedal

releases fluid but does not suck in air on the return stroke, but constant attention to the reservoir is still necessary. A more sophisticated version (Easi-bleed) has a large reservoir which sits on top of the normal one, and is pressurised, usually by a connection to the spare wheel. This leaves the operator free to open the valves and close them when the fluid flows without air bubbles.

HANDBRAKE

Mention has already been made of the handbrake, which on nearly every car acts on the rear wheels, expanding the brake shoes, or contracting the pads, usually mechanically by means of a cable but sometimes, especially on a live axle, by rods. Sometimes this is by means of Bowden cables, one to each wheel directly from the handbrake or a short rod linked to it, and sometimes by open cable running round guides.

Cables tend to stretch in use and there is provision for tightening them, but make sure before you do that you are not compensating for worn shoes or pads. If there is too

Fig. 9.18. Rear brake shoes. The lever is a part of the handbrake mechanism.

much movement of the handbrake (it should operate in three or four clicks of the ratchet) first check the state of the shoes before tightening the cables. There will be some method of achieving an equal pull on both brakes through a compensator, probably only a short lever or a crescent-shaped guide, which must be free and well lubricated with grease, especially as it is very vulnerable to the effects of road dirt. Bowden cables should have grease nipples on the outer conduit, and the mechanism of levers and clevis pins must be lubricated with white brake grease, if internal, or a molybdenum disulphide-based grease if external.

If the handbrake lever ratchet itself has suffered it may be possible to file new teeth onto it to restore it. Note, however, if you are not familiar with them, that some sports cars are fitted with fly-off handbrakes in which the ratchet is not engaged unless the button is pressed.

ABS BRAKING SYSTEMS

Many more recent vehicles are fitted with anti-lock braking systems. The stopping effect of the brakes of a vehicle is greatest when the wheels are revolving (providing they have grip), and it deteriorates if the wheels lock up. An ABS system will release the brake on a wheel that has locked (over about 3mph) and will reapply it once it is begun revolving again, continuing to do so as long as the pedal is depressed while the car is travelling at above the set minimum speed. By this means stopping distances are shortened and directional control of the car is maintained when braking on slippery surfaces.

The system operates by means of sensors on each of the wheels transmitting information to a computer. This operates a regulator valve to the wheel(s) as it begins to lock by reducing the pressure, and increasing it again as it begins to rotate again. The system has a high-pressure pump and is linked to the normal brake system.

Some earlier versions had mechanically-operated control systems incorporating belt-driven flywheels instead of the electronic controls now common.

Car braking systems that incorporate ABS are, of course, more complicated to work on than standard systems, though it's a job which is usually well within the scope of the amateur. But it is essential that you have the data relating to the particular model, so the relevant manual is a necessity.

Chapter 10

The engine

If you had the opportunity to drive the car before you took it to pieces you will have some idea of what the engine is like. If it pulled well, ran quietly, had a smoke-free exhaust, especially on the over-run, and did not consume vast quantities of oil you may not need to take it apart, but it is still worthwhile checking the compressions. This is done with a simple pressure gauge screwed or held into the spark plug hole, after the plug has been removed. Turn the engine slowly and watch the pressure build up until it reaches top dead centre (TDC). You should expect a reading of about 150psi (11 bar) on a normal engine. Wear will probably have reduced the ability of the piston and cylinder to hold full compression and a lower reading, of say 120-130psi (8-9bar) may be acceptable, but it is important that you get a fairly consistent reading from all the cylinders.

If all is well give the engine a thorough service (plugs, points, tappets, air and oil filters and oil change), put a small quantity of engine oil in each cylinder, put the plugs back loosely and mask the openings with tape. It may be some time before you use it but if you turn it over occasionally it will spread the oil on the surface of the bores and keep the piston rings lubricated.

If the compression readings were low it is worth taking the head off to check the valves and bores before deciding to take out the engine. In any event, with an unknown engine it is sensible to look inside it to check its condition.

While the head is off, remove and examine the valves and deal with them as detailed later.

If you need to undertake major work on the engine you'll have to remove it from the car. It is relatively easy if you have a radiator at the front that, when removed, leaves a gap, but less so if it has body panel work all round, especially if it is mid-mounted. Nearly all front-mounted engines are fitted and removed from above and the best way to do it is to use an engine hoist. Rear-mounted engines are usually slid out, supported by a trolley jack. Engine hoists are not particularly expensive but if you are only going to use it once it's better to hire one. The alternative is a simple block and tackle arrangement which, of course, needs a well placed beam above the car and space to roll the car out of the way when the engine

is lifted out. I have adopted this method for many years, using an inexpensive Haltrac system that has two sets of pulleys and nylon cord. I must say that I look at it in disbelief when the cords take the full weight of the engine (and gearbox), and I make sure that there is a wooden box directly below it in case they break, but it hasn't done yet. Of course, if the engine is small and light, two or three of your strongest friends may be able to manage it by hand while you direct operations.

A strong rope or chain should be passed round the engine at front and rear to act as a sling, though some engines have brackets bolted to the cylinder head to attach the lifting tackle to. If the front of the engine bay is closed off by body panels you will have to arrange for the engine and gearbox to adopt an extreme angle when being

Fig. 10.1. An engine hoist.

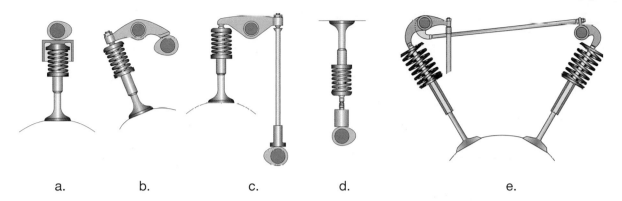

Fig. 10.2. Valve layouts. (a) overhead valves, single camshaft, bucket tappets; (b) overhead camshaft(s), with rockers; (c) overhead valves, pushrods; (d) side valves, with cam followers; (e) overhead valves, cross-over pushrods.

removed. With a very heavy engine, or when you are having to rely entirely on manpower to remove it, it's a good idea to lighten the load by removing as many components as possible, especially the gearbox.

Once out of the car most of us put the engine on a bench to work on it, but this is not entirely satisfactory as work needs to take place all over it and the better and more professional solution is to use an engine stand onto which the power unit is bolted at the clutch or drive end and which enables it to be rotated about its axis.

You will, of course, have disconnected and marked all wires connected to it (though more modern engines will have multi-pin plugs that cannot be wrongly connected) and the throttle and choke cables or linkages, exhaust system, pipes, water hoses and anything else that may impede its removal, and drained it of oil and water. Be especially careful with the fuel supply pipes, making sure that you disconnect them from as high up as possible to prevent the flow of fuel, and seal them well.

When the engine is removed it can be cleaned down thoroughly, using a degreasing agent and brush and then washing it off with water. After this the gearbox can be taken off, if you didn't have to do this prior to engine removal, and the engine can be mounted upright on its stand or on the bench.

Strip all the components from it, storing them complete and in boxes together with any wires or fittings such as gaskets, which you will probably not use again but will be useful as patterns. Note and write down anything odd or peculiar that might help in the rebuild, and if such things as engine mounting brackets are handed, label them. It all saves time and frustration later.

The methods by which the valves are operated, and the drive system, vary from engine to engine. On post-war cars the

Fig. 10.3. Some arrangements for driving camshafts. (a) gear train driving double camshafts; (b) chain driving single camshaft; (c) toothed belt driving double camshafts; (d) chain drive to side camshaft – push rods from there, or cam followers for side valves.

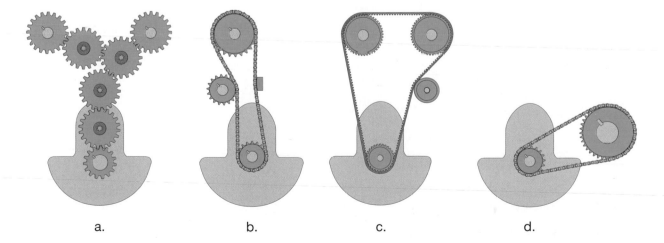

Fig. 10.4. A crankshaft nose, showing driving key and pulley for toothed timing belt.

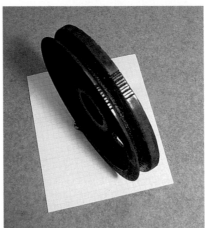

Far left: Fig. 10.5. A generator drive pulley from a crankshaft nose showing keyway.

Left: Fig. 10.6. A variety of timing marks on a drive pulley – the manual will tell you which is which.

Fig. 10.7. A 1934 MG M Type. The drive to this overhead is through the dynamo, mounted vertically in front, here removed for repair.

valves are nearly always found in the cylinder head but some may be in the block and a few cars, such as Rovers, Rolls-Royces and Bentleys, had the inlet valves in the head and the exhaust valves in the block.

Start by removing the timing cover, if it has one. This will involve the removal of the nut or bolt on the end of the crankshaft holding the pulley for the generator drive and the timing chain, gear or toothed-belt drive. This is sometimes very tight, and a well-fitting socket spanner with a long bar to give plenty of leverage may be required. But before removing the pulley you need to establish where the timing marks are situated.

The valves are required to begin their opening and closing movements at specific points in the cycle of events in relation to the position of the crankshaft. These are predetermined by the designer, and to aid assembly (and reassembly) marks are provided at the crankshaft and camshaft which are aligned when the No.1 piston is at the top of its compression stroke, either with each other or with stationary marks on the engine or timing case. On some engines with toothed driving belts, the stationary marks are moulded or cast into the timing cover and may consist of marks that align with notches in the crankshaft and camshaft pulleys (which are splined or keyed onto their respective shafts). Where the drive to the camshaft is by gear there may be marks, such as centre punch dots, on specific teeth that are meshed together, and chain-driven systems will probably have marks that face each other and need lining up with a ruler or straight edge.

Establish where they are, and if none exists, make some by setting No.1 piston at the very top of its stroke with both valves closed. Accurate valve timing is essential because if the sequence of valve events is not absolutely precise not only will the engine not run properly but considerable damage may be done by the valves striking the tops of the pistons.

If the camshaft lives in the cylinder block you can leave the drive undisturbed for the moment and work on removing the cylinder head. If the camshaft or shafts lie in the head, the drive to them (chain or belts) must be disconnected first; but in the case of chains check for wear by looking at the tensioning arrangements. If the tensioner is at full stretch, or more than about half way, then the chain will need replacing. A toothed belt has a finite life and as you will not know when it was last replaced the wisest move is to fit a new one, whatever the existing one looks like. They are much easier to replace with the engine out and usually lethal to the engine if they break in service.

Fig. 10.8. The MG M Type engine rebuilt.

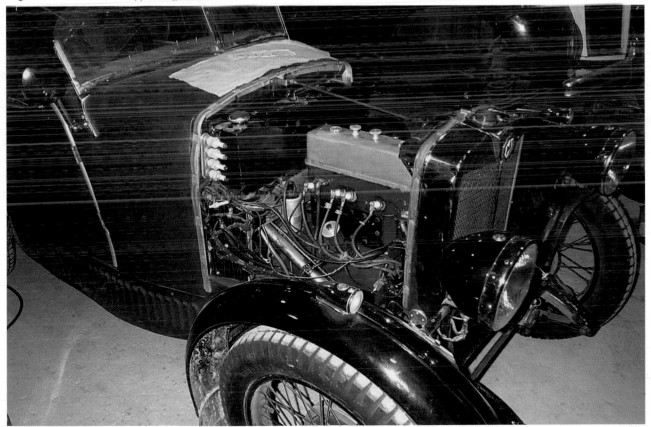

CYLINDER HEAD

To remove the head you may need to take off the rocker shaft, if any, or the camshaft(s) before you can get to the holding down nuts or bolts (but not on the example in Fig. 10.9). Remove the nuts or bolts, noting, in the case of bolts, whether any are longer than the others and which holes they belong in, and carefully lift the head.

If it is held down by nuts on studs through the head itself the job may prove difficult. Try tapping with a soft-faced hammer or with a piece of wood interposed between an ordinary hammer and the head. Some heads have lugs cast in the underside which can be gently tapped upwards, or you can put the starter motor back and try motoring it over. If all fails, a thin blade tapped into the edge of the gasket in several places (taking care not to mark the mating surfaces) should do the trick; and if it doesn't you will have to remove the crankshaft and pistons and tap a large piece of wood gently up each cylinder bore in turn.

With the head removed, inspect the surface and the gasket for any signs of leakage. Aluminium heads

Fig. 10.9. A cylinder head (Ford) complete with single camshaft.

especially can warp and allow coolant to leak out of the joint, or into adjacent cylinders. You will need a new cylinder head gasket and should note which side is to be placed next to the cylinder block – it is usually marked but if of the copper/asbestos type the beaded side goes downwards.

Remove the camshafts or rocker shaft if these have not already been taken off, and then the valves. There are normally two per cylinder, but recent engines often have four; there is no magic in this though as Bugattis had three and Bentleys had four in the 1920s.

Valves are usually held in place by two split cotters held in a groove in the valve stem by a collar which in turn holds the spring. It is necessary to compress the spring

Fig. 10.10. An aluminium cylinder head removed ready for reconditioning.

Fig. 10.11. A professional's spring compressor.

Fig. 10.12. Exhaust valves in block.

Fig. 10.13. Valves and springs carefully stored.

Fig. 10.14. The pair of valves on the left are badly burned and will need to be replaced.

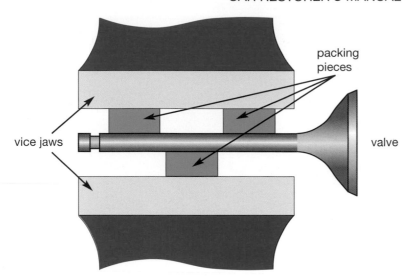

packing
pieces

vice jaws

valve

Fig. 10.15. Straightening a valve stem in a vice.

Fig. 10.16. An oil seal on a valve stem. These should be replaced.

to remove the cotters when the whole assembly can be taken apart and the valve slid out of its guide. Spring compressors are available for this purpose, most being of a simple screw clamp design, but professionals use a purpose built bench with a lever compressor.

Keep the valves and their associated components separate from each other and number them so that they can be replaced in their original locations. This is particularly important on overhead camshaft engines that have their tappet clearances adjusted by means of shims in the tops of 'buckets', since you will need to replace these in their original positions to regain the original clearances. If the tappets are hydraulic, store them in separate containers or compartments filled with clean oil to minimize oil loss from them.

Note that some cars, and especially performance cars, often have two or more springs per valve. It's always a good idea to fit new valve springs, but especially so if you are aware that the engine has been standing for some considerable time. They are not usually expensive and it is money well spent, bearing in mind the important part they play in the efficient running of the engine. Similarly, it is always a good idea to replace the valve stem oil seals.

Clean each valve stem and replace it in its guide. It should slide freely without side play or stickiness; side play means that the guide is worn and will need replacing – usually by pressing it out and the new one in – and if the valve is reluctant to slide freely its stem may be bent. Replacement is the best cure but if unobtainable you may be able to straighten it in a vice.

Clean the combustion chambers by carefully scraping away any carbon deposits, and inspect the valve seating in the head and on the valve itself. If either is badly pitted it will need refinishing, but in general lapping the two together with fine grinding paste will produce the

Fig. 10.17. A valve being ground.

required matt grey ring round each seat. To do this a small quantity of paste is smeared onto the seat and the valve partially rotated with the grinding tool (or screwdriver if the valve head is slotted) between the palms of the hands, while being pressed lightly against the head. Clean the paste off from time to time using paraffin and be careful not to get any in the guide; a light spring beneath the valve head helps speed up the process. If the seat is too far gone to clean up by lapping it will have to be reground – a simple operation for the engine refinisher who inserts a mandrel into the valve guide and then grinds the seat with a shaped abrasive wheel in a special electric drill. Similarly, if the valve itself is pitted, it can be ground to the correct angle.

Fig. 10.18. A mandrel inserted in a valve guide.

Fig. 10.19. A valve seat being ground.

Fig. 10.20. A mandrel inserted into an exhaust valve guide.

Above left: Fig. 10.21. The cutter is placed on the mandrel.

Above right: Fig. 10.22. Cutting the recess.

Left: Fig. 10.23. The recess cut to the correct depth.

Below: Fig. 10.24. The hardened steel insert.

Above left: Fig. 10.25. The insert is knocked into place.

Above right: Fig. 10.26. A 45° cutter for cutting the seat angle.

Right: Fig. 10.27. Ready for finish grinding.

If it hasn't already been done, this is the time to convert the engine to run on unleaded petrol, but it's a job for the engine repair specialist who will remove the exhaust valve seats in the head and replace them with hardened ones.

Again, a mandrel is inserted, this time into the exhaust valve guide to steer a cutter which prepares a housing for the hardened insert.

The cutter is rotated at a fairly slow speed to the exact depth of the insert. The insert, which is an interference fit (very slightly larger than its seating) is then pressed or knocked in (in the case of a cast-iron head). With aluminium heads the insert is refrigerated and the head warmed to 100°C so that the insert can be tapped lightly in.

It is then necessary to shape the insert to an angle of 45° to provide a seat for the valve. Again a mandrel is inserted and a suitable cutter used to produce the seat (Fig. 10.26) which is then finished with an abrasive wheel as in the refinishing process. Fig. 10.28 shows the finished result and Fig. 10.29 the before and after comparison on this Ford V6 engine.

Next, check the face of the cylinder head with a straight edge to ensure that it is not warped – if it is it will need skimming (milling or grinding flat) by a specialist, who will clamp it to the bed of a milling machine and shave a few thousands of an inch off.

If the camshaft(s) are in the head, check the bearings for wear by replacing the shaft in its bearings and seeing if there is any sideways play – the shaft should revolve freely without any play. If there is any significant play the bearings will need renewing.

Rockers are usually bushed and these bushes can be driven out and replaced. Take care when fitting the new ones to ensure that any oil feed holes in the bush align with those in the rocker itself. The rocker face which operates the valve should be smooth and

Fig. 10.28. The finished insert.

Fig. 10.29. Before (right) and after (left).

Fig. 10.30. A milling machine with cylinder head mounted on it.

Fig. 10.31. Facing the head.

Fig. 10.32. The sump is held to the block by a series of small bolts.

ENGINE BLOCK

Remove the sump and clean out the gunge from it and from the gauze, if it has one, and the oil pump. Undo each of the big-end bearings and gently push the piston/connecting rod assembly up out of the block replacing the lower half of the big end bearing loosely and ensuring that the assembly is numbered. This is usually done on the boss that holds the big-end bolt and may be a stamped number or filed marks, or centre punch dots, and if there is none present make some to correspond with the number of the cylinder bore, starting with 'one' at the timing end.

The main bearing caps, also marked, can now be released and the crankshaft removed complete with flywheel assembly, taking note of the bearing arrangement that locates the crankshaft longitudinally. This may be by means of loose half-round thrust

polished. If it is grooved or pitted it may be possible to stone it smooth, but rockers are often case hardened (i.e. hardened on the outside only) and if you take a lot off you will get down to the softer metal, and a replacement will then be necessary.

Clean everything thoroughly, paying particular attention to removing all traces of grinding paste, and clean and blow through any oilways and water passages, removing any sludge, rust particles and limescale, and reassemble the valvegear, lubricating the valve stems and guides plentifully.

On OHC engines with shim adjustment of tappet clearances, now is the time to set them by measuring with a feeler gauge and fitting shims of the appropriate value to give the required clearance.

Fig. 10.34. The crankshaft removed. The pistons and connecting rods will have to be pushed up the bores to remove them.

Fig. 10.33. The sump removed. The round gauze-covered oil pick-up is on the right with the delivery pipe to the oil pump top left. Note the five main bearing caps.

bearings that need recovering after noting their position, often at the centre main bearing but sometimes at the flywheel end.

Work can now begin on the cylinder block which should be cleaned and stripped of paint. Any cracks should be evident and the most likely place is on the outside of a water jacket (frost being the possible cause). If you find a crack it's possible to patch it using a mild steel or aluminium plate with small screws, closely set and tapped into the block with a layer of silicone sealer between patch and block. Welding is a possibility, but only for an expert as there's a danger of warping the block. If there is any internal damage this can be repaired by specialists but it's expensive and you may be better off looking for a replacement block.

Above: Fig. 10.35. Cylinder bore. The shiny part of the bore denotes the piston's travel. Note the 'land' at the top of the bore.

Right: Fig. 10.36. Half-round thrust bearings.

Below left: Fig. 10.37. Two core plugs are visible above the clutch (arrowed).

Below right: Fig. 10.38. A shell bearing and housing. Note the locating tab.

Examine the cylinder bores, which should be smooth and shiny and without any marks of any sort. At the very top of the bore you may find a raised portion running in a ring round the cylinder (the 'lip' or 'land'); this is the portion not contacted by the piston ring and is a good indicator of wear. If the 'land' is very pronounced then wear is considerable, and vice versa.

Should you find that the bores are marked or that there is a lot of wear, then a rebore will be

necessary, which in turn will automatically call for new pistons and rings. There is, though, a limit to how many times an engine can be rebored. Depending on condition it is normal to rebore in increments of ten thousandths of an inch as far as 40 thou, but some engines can be taken out to as much as 60 thou.

If it has already been bored out to its limit it will need to be resleeved, which will give you a standard-size bore again. Should this not be necessary, yet some bore wear exists, the fitting of new piston rings will most likely compensate for the wear. In such a case the 'land' at the top of the bore should be removed either by using a special tool or by carefully scraping it with a bearing scraper or the edge of an old piston ring. This will ensure that the new top ring is not damaged by coming into contact with it.

Although it may be thought that a highly polished bore is desirable it is in fact common practice to leave minute machining marks on the surface as these retain oil better than a polished bore. If you are not having a rebore, you can use a tool called a glaze-buster to remove the polished finish and introduce a minute degree of roughness to the bore.

If the camshaft is in the block this should be removed together with the cam followers (being kept separate from each other and marked for return to their respective places). Camshaft bearing surfaces should be examined as with the OHC variety and replaced as necessary. Cam followers should show no rubbed patches or excessive wear on the surface in contact with the cam. Pushrods should be replaced in their original locations and be checked for straightness, as a sticking valve or badly fitting valve cap could cause them to bend.

The block should now be thoroughly cleaned inside and out with particular attention paid to any oil ways which sometimes have screwed plugs (blanking plugs that can be removed to facilitate cleaning). It is surprising how much sludge can accumulate and all of it should be cleaned out. A good deal can be removed by use of a bottle brush and degreasing agent.

Water passages and main water galleries also need attention as years of operation with unfiltered water, old anti-freeze and particles of rust combine to form sludge, usually accumulating at the lowest point in the system and building up from there. Over time this solidifies and becomes impervious to flushing out, even with chemicals, so you need to poke it out with a screwdriver and a stiff bent wire. Some engines have plates on the side of the cylinder block which on removal give access to the water passages and spaces between the cylinders, while others may have large screwed bungs or pressed-in plugs (see Fig. 10.37) in the engine block casting to facilitate access to the main water passages. A hole drilled into a core plug followed by a twist with a screwdriver will extract it, and new ones won't cost much. Use a smear of silicone sealant when inserting the replacements. If they are domed, fit them with the domed side outwards and tap the raised portion lightly to flatten them and ensure that their edges slot into the machined groove in the casting. Flanged plugs are a light push fit into their housings and are fitted with the flange outwards. Whatever provision is made, try to remove all deposits and thoroughly flush the whole system with water afterwards to clear out the loose debris.

Examine the crankshaft journals, both the big ends and mains, for wear and scoring and check each with its respective bearings. The shell bearings should be a matt grey in colour (see Fig. 10.38). If they have shiny patches or score marks they must be discarded and the crankshaft journals reground undersize to fit new oversize bearings. Crankshafts are normally ground in increments of ten thousandths of an inch, and up to three thousandths (-0.003in) is possible. If, before dismantling it, you had been able to drive the car (or at least run the engine) and had noticed low oil pressure, then worn crankshaft bearings would be the most likely cause.

The pistons and connecting rods can now be dealt with. If you are not replacing the pistons and there is no appreciable wear in the little end bearing (some side-to-side movement is acceptable but there should be no sideways play) you will not need to separate them, but

Fig. 10.39. Piston rings, showing the three parts of the oil control ring ('scraper') which returns surplus oil through slots in the piston.

Fig. 10.40. A piston and connecting rod assembly.

Fig. 10.41. The piston has an arrow on the crown, facing the camera, to show that it faces the front of the engine. The connecting rod has a large 'F' for the same purpose.

if you do, look carefully to see how the gudgeon pin is retained in the piston or rod. On older engines it may not be retained at all, being of the fully-floating variety when it will have soft metal end pads to prevent scoring of the bore, or it may have circlips in grooves at each end In the piston. If nothing is visible, look inside the piston as the pin may be clamped to the little end, or possibly to the piston, by screws. If none of these methods is used it will be an interference fit in the piston. Try heating the top of the piston above the gudgeon pin in boiling water and tapping the pin out with a drift. If this fails you will have to visit an engine specialist with equipment for heating to the correct temperature and pushing the pin out. Take your new pistons and let him do both jobs together.

Piston rings are made of very brittle cast iron and do not like being bent, so to remove and refit them use three strips of very thin metal slid under each ring, taking off one at a time. Before fitting new rings to old pistons make sure that the grooves are clean. There is often a peg in each groove which locates the ring, ensuring that the ring gaps are radially disposed; if there aren't any, ensure that the gaps do not coincide when you fit

the new rings and check them (though these have probably been machined to size) with a feeler gauge. On water-cooled engines the gaps should be about .002in per inch diameter of cylinder bore and about double this for an air-cooled engine. To make the measurement, slide the ring on top of a piston inside the cylinder and ensure that it is square to the bore by sitting it on the piston crown. Instructions regarding fitting the new rings will be included in their packaging.

Pistons, and sometimes connecting rods, are marked to ensure that they are positioned correctly, the mark usually denoting the front or timing end of the engine (see Fig. 10.41). Using plenty of oil, the pistons may now be fitted into their respective bores. This is usually done from the top but on older engines the bore may be too narrow to accept the big end, so in such cases the pistons are entered from the bottom and there is usually a tapered lead-in on the bottom of the bore to facilitate this. The rings will need to be compressed to allow them to slide in and special ring compressors are available for this purpose. However, a suitably shaped piece of thin metal strip

may be used instead, or a worm-drive clip with three slips of metal underneath it held just tight enough (see Fig. 10.42), but not so as to prevent the movement on the piston as it is gently tapped into the cylinder with the handle of a hammer or a soft-faced mallet.

Fig. 10.42. Replacing the piston; compressing the rings.

metal strips

piston

worm drive clip

Fig. 10.43. The three clutch components – pressure plate (cover), driven plate and release (thrust) bearing.

Before refitting the crankshaft, clean its internal oilways thoroughly, if necessary using a piece of soft metal (brass or aluminium) to remove any hardened, carbonized deposits. As it revolves the crankshaft acts as a centifruge and tends to leave hardened deposits on the walls of the oilways which can very considerably restrict the flow of oil.

When refitting the shaft, oil the bearing surfaces liberally and ensure that the bearing shells are replaced correctly with the small tabs in the right place. If the thrust bearings are of the loose variety and not built into one of the bearing caps, these also need positioning correctly. The nuts or bolts need tightening to the specified torque and locked with whatever device (if any) is used on your particular engine. It makes sense to turn the crankshaft over two or three times when each bearing has been tightened to ensure that none is too tight.

At this point, if you have not already stripped the crankshaft completely, the clutch should be unbolted from the flywheel and inspected. Normally wear takes place on the driven plate and on the thrust release bearing, and it is a good idea to replace these two

Fig. 10.44. An older pattern clutch with separate springs instead of diaphragm spring.

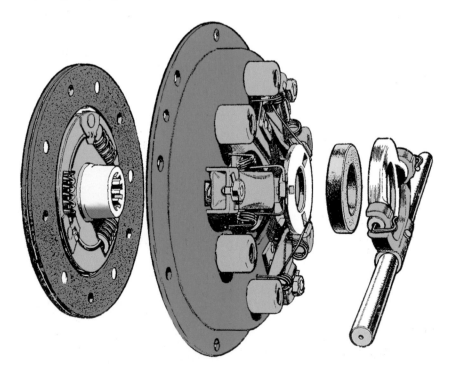

items while they are accessible. The clutch pressure plate should be inspected for scoring and replaced if any is present. If its face is in good condition the flywheel need not be removed from the crankshaft (unless the starter ring needs attention), but if there are signs of wear and scoring it will have to be refaced, which is a job for a machine shop or engine specialist.

When reassembling the clutch, the driven plate needs aligning accurately with the bearing for the gearbox drive shaft. The bolts holding the pressure plate or cover are left slightly loose and an aligning tool is inserted in the bearing in the end of the crankshaft which centralises the plate, when the bolts can be tightened.

The tool is merely a short length of metal or even wood which is turned to the two diameters, bearing and splines, on which the driven plate is located. Universal plastic tools for this purpose are now easily and cheaply available.

The thrust race on older cars will probably be a carbon block, and on later cars a ball race.

The starter ring gear tends to wear only in certain places as an engine usually comes to rest in the same place each time, and it is there that engagement with the starter motor takes place. If the wear is excessive the ring gear, which is a shrink fit, can be replaced or even moved around the periphery of the flywheel to allow engagement to take place on an unworn portion, or of course you may be able to rotate the flywheel to achieve the same result.

To remove the ring gear for replacement, put the flywheel on a bench, drill a hole between two gear teeth and then split the ring with a cold chisel. It will then come free and can be taken off the flywheel. Polish the replacement in three equally spaced places, heat evenly all round, preferably on a metal plate with a gas torch, until the polished areas change colour

from purple to dark blue. This temperature should be held for about five minutes when the ring will have expanded sufficiently to slip over the register on the flywheel. Final seating can be helped by a few light taps with a soft-faced mallet, before leaving it to cool.

If you are merely repositioning it, it will need heating evenly all round to loosen it when it can be tapped off the flywheel, and then dealt with as above, but remember to mark the new position on the ring and flywheel first.

If the oil pump is in the sump it should be checked before refitting by removing the bottom plate and inspecting it for wear. There are two normal types of pump in use, those that have two gear wheels and those that have two rotors (Fig. 10.45). Wear can take place between the gears and the inside of the case and the only remedy is to replace the pump. If the end-plate is worn it may be possible to restore it by lapping it on a plate with fine emery cloth, but the wear is probably caused by excessive end play which will continue to wear the plate, so again a replacement is desirable.

Associated with the pump is the oil pressure relief valve which is usually situated in the engine block in an oil gallery. If you have not already cleaned out this system, it should be done now.

The relief valve consists either of a spring-loaded ball bearing or plunger and it is important to ensure that whichever you have is in good condition. If not, the plunger can be lapped to its seat like the valves, using fine carborundum paste, or metal polish if it only needs cleaning up. If it's a ball type, a replacement ball (of the same size) should be fitted, and this can be tapped lightly onto its seat to ensure a good seal. Check that the spring is not broken, and when replacing the adjusting screw return it to its original position. You can adjust the oil pressure with the engine running later.

Fig. 10.45. A two-rotor oil pump.

Refit the pump and its pipe and fit a new gasket to the sump, being particularly careful with the arrangements over the crankshaft seals. Pressed steel sumps are often indented slightly where they are bolted up to the block and these should be tapped down level with the surface of the flange in order to provide a sound, oil-tight seal.

The head may now be fitted together with its new gasket. The bolts, or nuts if it is held down by studs, need to be tightened down progressively, starting in the middle, in a spiral so that the head is, as it were, spread across the block. It should be torqued down to whatever value is specified in the manual; some are merely torqued to a given value while others require further tightening through a number of degrees which will be specified. The camshaft drive arrangement can now be connected, bearing in mind what was mentioned earlier about timing marks.

If for any reason there are no visible marks and you omitted to make any when dismantling you will have to resort to the old-fashioned method of using a timing diagram but for this you

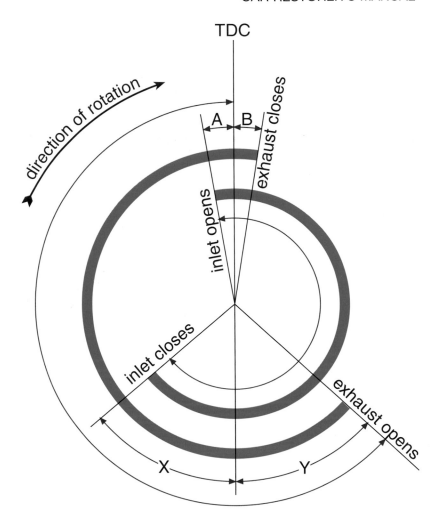

Fig. 10.46. A timing diagram.

need to know at what point the valves open.

Prepare a diagram as in Fig. 10.46 on a piece of stiff cardboard to fit on the nose of the crankshaft, and make a reference mark on the crankcase. As the individual cams are integral with the camshaft you will need to time only the inlet valve of No.1 cylinder if there is only a single camshaft, or this and the exhaust valve of No.1 cylinder if there are two camshafts. Although the chart shows the closing point of the valves this is for checking and information only, there is nothing you can do to alter it as the cam profiles are already formed on the shaft.

First set the inlet (and exhaust if there are two camshafts) tappet clearance to the specified value, turn the crankshaft until No.1 piston is at top dead centre (TDC) and align this point on the diagram with the reference mark you made and ensure that the diagram is locked tight and cannot slip. With the drive disconnected, turn the crankshaft backwards (against the direction of rotation) the few degrees necessary to achieve the value A in the diagram. This is done at the flywheel by using the formula: diameter of flywheel multiplied by 3.14 divided by 360.

This will give you the amount (in inches or millimetres depending which you used) to mark on the flywheel rim, by which it should be turned backwards. Adjust the camshaft until the No.1 inlet cam has just made contact with its follower or rocker and is about to start opening the valve. Connect the drive, making sure that there is no slack in the drivetrain, belt or chain and that the tensioner is properly adjusted.

Now turn the crankshaft through two complete revolutions (720°) and check the valve events with reference to the diagram. The timing of each engine type is specified by the designer, and the timing of the opening and closing of the valves will depend on a variety of factors to produce the power and torque characteristics required. In the diagram shown, the values of A and B will each be about 5° and X and Y about 45° for an engine of reasonable power output, but as the opening and closing points of the inlet and exhaust valves do not need to be symmetrical the values are not necessarily the same for all engines.

The period when both the inlet and exhaust valves are both open (the value of A+B) is known as overlap. On an engine of low or moderate power output there may be none, with the inlet valve opening at or even after TDC, whereas on a sports or racing engine it may be quite considerable – the racing version of the famous K3 MG had the inlet valve opening 45° before TDC and an overlap of 81°.

When the timing arrangements have been satisfactorily completed, rotate the engine to ensure that all is well and that there are no untoward noises, and complete the fitting up of the timing case, crankshaft pulley, etc. using new seals and gaskets as necessary. When complete it can be painted with a heat resistant engine paint (available in a limited range of colours). Now, cover any openings with masking tape, put a good squirt of oil in each cylinder, screw the plugs in loosely and store the engine in a safe place or put it back into the chassis.

Chapter 11

The cooling system

The vast majority of cars are water-cooled, though there are a few – such as the VW Beetle, Porsches and 2CV Citroën – that are air-cooled. Air cooling is the simpler method, and there are none of the corrosion or freezing problems that water-cooled systems face. However, a water cooling system keeps the engine at a more constant temperature, allowing closer tolerances, and it provides a useful way of quietening some at least of the engine noise. The lubrication system also affords some cooling as the circulating oil carries off heat, some of which is dissipated by the air stream flowing over the sump, and through the oil cooler when fitted. Some air-cooled engines, notably that of the 2CV, rely on this to cool the exhaust valves, which allows flat-out running without overheating.

The typical water-cooled system consists of a water jacket around the cylinders and, more important, the cylinder head where the heat is generated, and a radiator (which is in fact a heat exchanger, the coolant flowing through many narrow channels that are in contact with the air stream that in turn carries off the heat). Early cars relied on the thermo-syphon system, whereby the hot water rises and flows into the top of the radiator before being cooled, and with increasing density moves to the bottom and then back up into the engine in a continuous cycle. Later a water pump and/or fan were added to ensure a more positive flow of water in the system and a more effective flow of air through the radiator, especially when the normal flow is reduced through the car moving slowly (e.g. in traffic) or stops altogether through coming to rest.

In restoring a car it is necessary to ensure that the flow of both water and air is as unrestricted as possible. We have already dealt with the water passages within the cylinder block and head in the last chapter, so we can turn straightaway to the radiator. This needs to be removed to clean it properly. On some older cars the radiator is attached to the ornamental shell and may in fact form a part, being soldered to it. If this is the case it is worthwhile trying to devise an alternative system since the removal of the radiator core from the shell each time either needs attention adds to the cost if it has to be done professionally. On more modern cars it is held to the front body pressing by bolts and/or tongues that slip into rubber housings.

You can test the radiator for leaks by blanking either the inlet or outlet and, with a piece of old inner tube (complete with its valve), blanking off the other, then pressurizing it slightly with a foot pump (not more than about 5psi)

Fig. 11.1. A wax type thermostat.

Fig. 11.2. A convoluted water hose.

Fig. 11.3. A worm drive clip with heat shrink tubing.

Fig. 11.4. A replacement water pump.

immersing it in water to see whether there are any leaks.

Many radiators are made of copper and a leak in the matrix can be repaired quite easily by soldering. However, the aluminium radiators you are likely to find on sports and racing cars are definitely a job for a specialist.

If you find leaks in a copper radiator, mark them and, after drying, thoroughly prepare the areas to be soldered by scraping away the paint down to bare metal. Solder the damaged area using a soldering iron, as a blowlamp is likely to spread heat and may damage other soldered seams. There are numerous specialists who can repair or re-core radiators, or even make new ones should this be necessary.

The inside of the radiator can be flushed out with a hose pipe connected to the bottom outlet (this will push water against the normal flow of coolant and will help to dislodge any sediment that may be present). Clean the outside of the radiator by spraying it with a jet of water through the matrix and dry it with compressed air, after which it can be sprayed with matt black paint.

Water pumps may be completely separate units or built into the cylinder block. Units may be repairable, using new bearings and seals, or merely replaceable (Fig. 11.4). Older separate units that have been standing for any length of time tend to suffer badly from corrosion in the body and may have seized bearings. If yours is too old for a replacement to be available, and you cannot source a spare one, you will have to send it to a specialist for rebuilding or, if desperate, you may find a substitute that you can adapt at your local marina or yacht chandler. It may be expensive but it will be bronze and impervious to most forms of corrosion.

Fans used to be belt driven and were often attached to the water pump itself, but eventually

Fig. 11.5. A viscous coupled fan. Note the irregular spacing of the blades.

designers, searching for better fuel consumption, realised that a fan absorbed power and was unnecessary for much of the time when the car was in motion. Viscous couplings were designed which permitted the fan to operate only when the temperature reached a predetermined figure, and subsequent to this came the electrically-operated device with which we are all familiar, which is activated by a sensor in the coolant and hot wired (that is, not through the ignition circuit) so that it can run when the engine temperature rises immediately after being switched off.

If your fan is metal it deserves a repaint, or a polish if it is aluminium. Do not be surprised if the blades are oddly spaced (see Fig. 11.5) or if one is twisted more than the others; they are designed like this to try to quieten the air flow.

Many engines are only marginally cooled and there is usually provision in the cowling that houses the electric fan for the fitting of a second one which will be required if extra demands are made on the engine such as air-conditioning or towing. If yours is undercooled you can fit a second fan to help the original one, but make sure first that the system is thoroughly clean and serviceable. Otherwise you will be curing the symptoms and not the fault.

One of the causes of overheating, especially on older cars with narrow bonnets and powerful engines, is that there is insufficient ventilation of the engine compartment, and it is on record that on one MG model attention to this reduced the underbonnet temperature by 20°F. I have on occasion put louvres into bonnets to help get the heat away from the engine compartment.

Another prime cause of overheating is the thermostat. This is normally fitted into the bottom, (cylinder head end), of the top hose and is designed to close off the coolant circulation through the radiator until it has reached operating temperature. There are two types, a bellows pattern which when it fails should fail safe (i.e. open, so that the engine takes longer to reach operating temperature but does not overheat), or a wax type that is not designed to fail safe. The bellows type often does not fail safe either and, like the wax type, when it fails, closes the circuit and causes almost instant overheating, so if your car suffers from this, the first suspect (apart from the fan belt, if any) should be the thermostat.

Thermostats come in different heat ranges and can be tested by suspending them in water in a vessel which has a source of heat, and by means of a thermometer you will be able to see at what temperature the valve begins to open. Some people merely throw them away when faulty and never replace them, but this means more wear on the engine when cold, and no heater for a long time on cold mornings.

The rubber hoses should be replaced as a matter of course. If the correct ones are not available you will have to look for something similar or use the convoluted variety which can be bent to suit most needs (see Fig. 11.2). Worm-drive clips should be used to secure them – stainless steel ones are available and look good under the bonnet. The ends of this type of clip are often rather sharp and can easily damage hands or cleaning cloths, but can be cut short once fitted and covered with a short length of heat shrink tubing which tidies them up and renders them harmless (see Fig. 11.3).

When filling the system do not forget to add the recommended quantity of anti-freeze or inhibitor, especially with aluminium engines or engines with aluminium heads, to prevent future corrosion, and remember to drain and change it every two years or so, using soft rain water if available.

Fill the system slowly and check for air locks, especially in the heater circuit which should be on, and after running the engine check the level several times. Filling used to be straight into the header tank on top of the radiator but for many years this has been detached from the radiator and sits where convenient in the engine compartment. Cooling systems are designed to work under pressure – anything between 7-15psi – and the rating should be marked on the cap. If it's necessary to replace it, one of the same value should be used. There is often an expansion tank with a tube which runs from just under the cap, so that when the pressure is exceeded the valve in the cap opens and the coolant escapes to the tank from which it is returned by vacuum when the engine cools.

Air-cooled engines rely on fans to blow air over the cylinders and heads which have cooling fins to help dissipate the heat. Some of these, especially with rear-engined configurations where there is no natural air flow, as on the Porsche, are quite massive, and it is important that the drive belt and bearings are in good condition otherwise disaster can strike quickly. Release the belt and inspect it closely for cracks, replacing it if any doubt exists at all, and try the bearings for any end or sideways play.

Air is directed over the fins by means of baffles made of pressed steel which if loose can create unwanted rattles. The airflow is usually drawn through a mesh to keep out extraneous objects that might damage the fan blades; check that this is intact and clean it and the spaces between the cooling fins so that there is maximum contact between the metal and the cooling air.

Oil coolers are miniature radiators and often suffer from damage by being placed low down where they are subject to impact from stones and road debris, bending the cooling fins. These can be straightened with a pair of long-nosed pliers, and the inside can be flushed out with paraffin.

Chapter 12

The fuel system

There are so many different carburettor types and fuel injection systems that what follows can only be somewhat basic and general, and if you are working on a car made after about 1970 then you will find the appropriate workshop manual invaluable.

The tank holding the petrol must be well supported as, when full, it can be very heavy. A gallon of petrol weighs about 10lb (4.5k), so ten gallons weighs 100lb (45kg), and on top of this is the weight of the tank itself. On cars with separate chassis, tanks are sometimes subject to flexing loads, and careful mounting is essential if leaks from mounting points are to be avoided; any rubber insulation should be carefully inspected to make sure that it has not hardened with age and can still perform its function. If necessary it should be replaced.

Because of the positioning of tanks and the water contained in the petrol, old tanks have a propensity to rust and are easily damaged by stones or other objects thrown up by the wheels, which is why early cars with exposed tanks were often lagged with strips of wood.

If your tank is damaged, it is better to either send it away for repair or to find a better one. It must be recognised that attempting to repair petrol tanks is dangerous. Empty tanks that have stood for many years, even though vented to atmosphere, often have residues that create gas when heated which then causes an explosion with dire results to the tank and usually also to the

operator. The following account, written by a highly experienced professional engineer, appeared in the Rolls-Royce Enthusiasts Club Bulletin in 1999 headed 'Tips for Healthy Living'.

The car '... had probably not had petrol put in its tank since about 1939. It had then been dieselized for many years, with great holes cut in the tank for a kingsize filter, an even bigger aircraft fuel gauge and a sophisticated pressure regulating valve.

It had then had a bulldozer blade through the top, and had stood outside for unknown time, the tank full of rain water, rusting away until holes appeared at the bottom and all the water ran out, leaving internal tide marks of rust. After which it was dry-stored in airy conditions.

'Not unreasonably, it was thought that 60 years after it last saw petrol it would be safe to open it up for repair, using a flame. Nevertheless, it was approached cautiously, in the open air, with a tentative flame around all the nooks and crannies. All went well, rivets ground off, seams unsoldered, bits all over the shop – until the last lap.

'The bosses in the ends of the tank, and which support it, are on the ends of plugged tubes, capped, pinned and soldered, fastened to diaphragms inside the tank. All joints and pins sound, no crack, no rust, no holes. On opening up, between them they held about three-quarters of a pint of genuine 1920s unleaded petrol.

'No explosion. No drama. No obituaries. Not this time. But the

tank had not held petrol for 60 years. Nor do I know how the petrol got in initially, for the tubes were intact and even during generous and cavalier heating to unsolder the structure there was no hint of seepage, not the slightest whiff of petrol...'

The message therefore is if the tank needs repair, let the specialists deal with it; they take great pains to ensure safety.

If, however, you are determined to have a go yourself you must ensure that no naked flame will be used on the tank and, if you need to solder it, that the soldering iron is heated a long way from it. Tanks are usually made from tinned mild steel sheet and soldered together and some of the larger ones may have riveted seams and baffles. Remove and drain it before you attempt the repair.

Cracks and damaged areas can be cut out and patched and seams resoldered. You will need a large soldering iron in order to retain the heat and the area must be very clean. All paint and rust should be removed and the metal treated with emery cloth until you finish up with a bright bare metal surface. If applying a patch this should be of mild steel similarly cleaned, and both surfaces need to be tinned. This is done by first coating the areas with flux and melting solder on to it with the iron, heated until the copper bit turns the flame green, until there is an even coating.

The patch is then placed on the tank with another coating of flux between them and the two heated together by the iron, more solder being fed into the edges. Seams should be cleaned in the same way, and if opened up they should be carefully tapped together before soldering. Surplus flux (the liquid variety is corrosive) should be washed off with hot water, and when dry the repair painted over.

Minor seepage and leaks can be dealt with less drastically by the use of proprietary chemical preparations which are swilled around the interior of the tank before drying and becoming a permanent sealant. They are advertised in the motoring magazines devoted to classic cars.

The pipe conveying the petrol to the pump should, of course, be in good condition and well supported throughout its length. Keep it well away from the exhaust, both for safety reasons and to prevent vaporization of the fuel. If there is a filter make sure that this is clean, and empty any sediment out of it.

Some later cars will have evaporative control systems to prevent the evaporation of fuel from the tank causing pollution. When stationary, evaporation of the fuel is taken care of by an activated carbon canister which absorbs it, and when running, air is drawn through the canister, which purges it into the inlet manifold. Depending on the model the filter may be due for renewal about every 12,000 miles (20,000km) in the absence of any other recommendation, or the complete canister itself replaced every 50,000 miles (80,000km).

Some curious arrangements for indicating the level of petrol in the tank have existed in the past, ranging from a simple dip stick or cork floats on twisted rods with an indicator on the tank filler cap to manometers on the dashboard. However, for many years fuel gauges have been electrically operated by means of a potentiometer activated by a float, the sender unit being fitted inside the tank (see Fig. 12.1). The information is transmitted to the

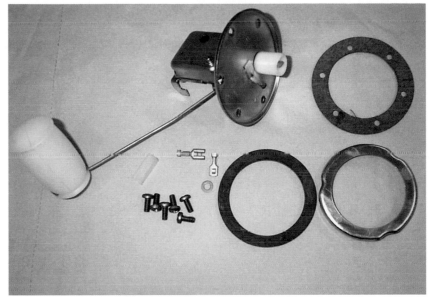

Fig. 12.1. A fuel tank sender.

gauge which operates by one of two methods (constant field or a bimetallic strip) and if replacement is necessary one of the same type should be used. (See Figs. 12.2 and 12.3.)

The electric fuel pump is dealt with in Chapter 14, but many cars have mechanical pumps almost invariably operated by a cam on the camshaft, either directly or by means of a short push rod. Like the electric version, these have a diaphragm and valves (see

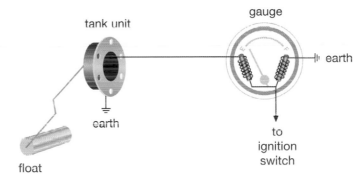

Fig. 12.2. A constant field fuel gauge.

Fig. 12.3. A bi-metallic strip fuel gauge.

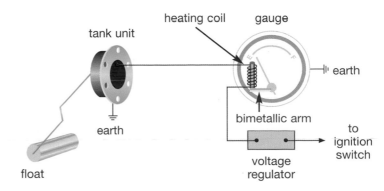

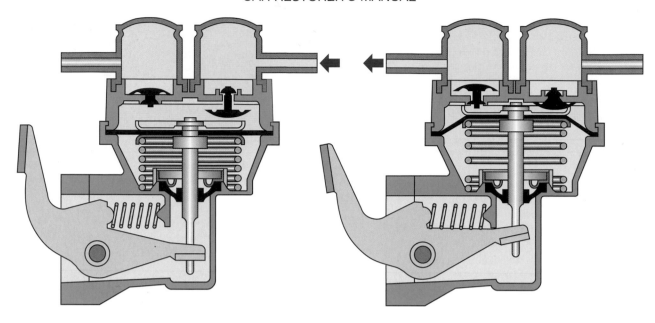

Fig. 12.4. A mechanical fuel pump. Left – priming; right – delivering.

Fig. 12.4). Fuel is sucked into the chamber when the diaphragm is flexed by the linkage to the camshaft through the inlet valve. Petrol is fed to the carburettor under pressure from a spring which is calibrated to ensure that it meets the carburettor's requirements in terms of fuel supply.

Many of these pumps can be dismantled so that the valves may be inspected and cleaned and the gauze filter checked. The diaphragm is removed, if necessary, by pressing it down in the centre against the pressure of the spring and turning it to unhook it from the actuating lever.

CARBURETTORS

There are and have been many types of carburettor, some made by car manufacturers themselves specifically for their own vehicles but most made by specialist firms. Whatever the make, they fall into one of two categories depending on their method of operation, either constant choke or constant vacuum.

CONSTANT CHOKE

Early carburettors were very much like a scent spray in which a column of air, caused by the vacuum created in the cylinder as the piston descends, flows over a jet which is in turn connected to a petrol supply; the air picking up petrol from the jet and intermingling with it to form a gas. Later it was realised that this provided for only one condition of the engine and that its requirements varied with speed, load, etc. As they became more sophisticated,

Fig. 12.5. A Weber twin-choke carburettor.

Fig. 12.6. The double float controlling the fuel supply in a Weber carburettor.

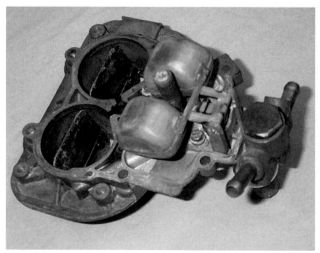

Fig. 12.7. The float chamber and jets of a Weber carburettor.

end of a long inlet tract, largely because fuel tanks were mounted on the scuttle and the flow of petrol was by gravity, but as rear-mounted tanks and pumps of varying types (or pressure from the exhaust!) were used to supply the carburettor these were re-sited onto the inlet manifold. For many years they tended to be of the updraught variety.

With so many different types of carburettor you will have to consult your manual to be able to follow the sequence of dismantling and assembly in detail, but if you do not have a manual, the following will guide you through it.

Undo the throttle and choke linkages and the feed pipe, and unbolt the carburettor from the manifold; if it is one of a pair you will need to remove the linkages that connect them together but do so by removing the clevis pins or other fixings to preserve the adjustment of the rods or cables (see Fig. 12.8).

carburettors incorporated other jets and air passages to compensate for different conditions, and a simple mechanism (the choke, or strangler as it used to be called) was introduced to close off most of the air supply in order to provide a richer mixture for starting. Later still a small pump was added to squirt extra fuel into the air stream to enrich the mixture in order to improve acceleration.

On early cars the carburettor tended to be fitted low down on the

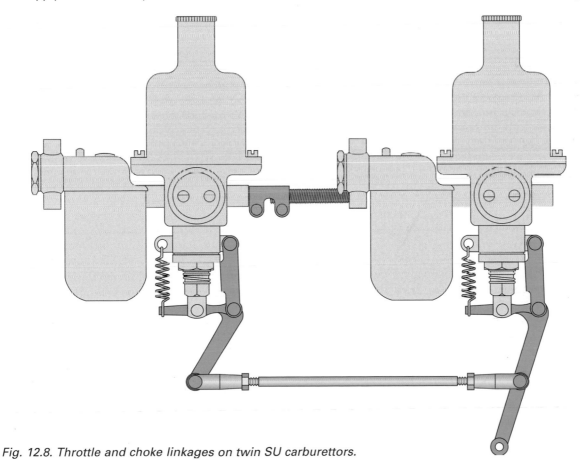

Fig. 12.8. Throttle and choke linkages on twin SU carburettors.

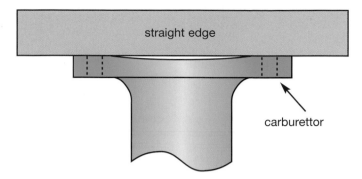

Fig. 12.9. Checking a carburettor flange for straightness.

Fig. 12.10. The bi-metallic coil that operates the automatic choke.

As there are few moving parts on this type of carburettor very little wear takes place apart from on the throttle spindle and its bushes. After thoroughly cleaning the outside, check to see whether any play exists in the spindle; if there is any appreciable movement it will be difficult to achieve good slow running as air will enter at this point when the butterfly itself is closed. The remedy is, of course, to renew the spindle and bushes; depending on age and make replacements may be available. If you do replace this assembly, be very careful when fitting the butterfly to ensure that it is the right way round, and after fitting the screws tap the ends gently to distort them slightly, or centre punch them, to prevent them unscrewing, but support the heads to avoid bending the spindle.

Modern instruments are sometimes quite complex and you should make detailed notes and sketches of the various components as you dismantle, particularly with regard to washers which may be aluminium, fibre or steel. Screws that have a spring under their heads are intended to be adjustable and it pays to count the number of turns as you unscrew them so that you can return them to their original settings. More modern carburettors have their mixture adjusting screws sealed by means of a wax type compound that needs removing before you can gain access to the screw.

Remove the top of the float chamber and carefully take out the spindle that holds the lever operating the fuel inlet valve. If this does not seat properly and so does not cut off the flow when the float reaches its proper level the engine will run rich and there may be leakage from the float chamber. Replace it if necessary, or if it is metal, lap it in to its seat using metal polish until there is a distinct ring all the way around it and the seat. Some petrols leave a gummy deposit, and if the needle sticks a treatment with one of the proprietary carburettor cleaners will remove the gum.

If the float is made of brass, shake it to see whether it contains petrol; if it does, it has a leak and the remedy is to place it in hot water which will extract the petrol and also show where the hole is. When dry the hole can be repaired by soldering, but be sparing with the solder or the float will increase in weight unnecessarily. Many modern floats are made of plastic which does not easily puncture, but check anyway.

It is worthwhile checking that the mounting flanges of both the carburettor and the manifold are straight by putting a steel rule across them (see Fig. 12.9). There is a tendency for the carburettor flange, especially, to bow so much that the gap is not fully taken up by the gasket and consequently allows air to be drawn in, thereby weakening the mixture and sometimes making starting difficult – careful filing will restore it.

Empty the gunge that is in the bottom of the float chamber and wash it out with clean petrol. The various jets can be removed and inspected. They should be blown through with a blast of compressed air and not poked out with a piece of wire; they are made of brass which is easily scratched and this will enlarge the jets and alter the characteristics of the carburettor. All the passages in the carburettor body should also be blown through and treated if necessary with cleaner to dissolve any deposits.

Rebuild carefully, using new washers and O rings if possible and, if you have the data available, check the setting of the fuel inlet valve which should shut off completely when the fuel is at or just below the level of the top of the main jet.

Some instruments are fitted with automatic chokes which may be electrically operated or which have a simple bi-metallic coil which reacts to heat. These have frequently been troublesome and when new, they were often replaced with over-riding manual controls. The electric type can be switched from the dashboard, with a tell-tale light, by eliminating the sensor, and with a small amount of ingenuity in making a bracket, the bi- metal coil system can be replaced with an ordinary choke cable.

If you do not intend to re-fit the carburettor to the engine immediately, put it in a polythene bag to keep it clean; if you do re-fit it, until you need to start the engine, tape over the end of the choke tube to prevent dirt getting in.

CONSTANT VACUUM

A carburettor depends on the air-flow through the choke tube and a fuel jet to make it function. Too large a choke tube and air-flow will suffer at slow speed, too small and performance at the top of the range will be adversely affected. Modern carburettors, as mentioned above, have compensation devices built in to provide the best compromise, but a different approach is taken by some instruments which vary the choke size depending on the demands of the engine.

The SU and Stromberg types meter the supply of petrol by means of a tapered needle working in a jet, the needle being connected to a piston or diaphragm that rises or falls under the influence of the vacuum in the inlet manifold, which also controls the air-flow in the choke tube.

There are many variants to suit different cars but the working principle is the same. The SU type responds to vacuum differences acting on a suction disc (Fig. 12.11) and the Stromberg by means of a diaphragm surrounding the piston (Fig. 12.12).

Burlen Fuel Systems (see Appendix), who have manufactured these carburettors since 1984, can restore or completely rebuild them and also offer spare parts and rebuild kits for them. If you intend to rebuild your own it is best to start with a complete kit of spares.

The following procedures refer specifically to the SU H-type carburettor, but other types are similar.

Remove and clean the carburettor externally, loosely screwing the banjo bolt and washers and filter assembly back into the float chamber lid for security, and also the connections for throttle and choke control. Part the float chamber by undoing the large retaining bolt at its base, again being careful to retain the washers. Remove the lid, noting the position of the drain pipe (if

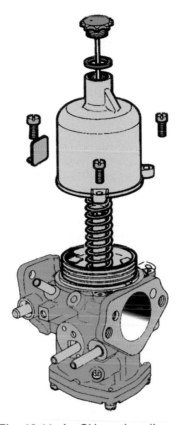

Fig. 12.11. An SU suction disc.

fitted), to gain access to the fuel inlet valve and deal with this, the float and the inside of the chamber as noted above.

When you replace the needle and forked lever, check the fuel level by inserting a rod, or drill of 7/16in (11mm) diameter underneath the curved forked lever and the edge of the lid. The lever should just touch the bar and can be carefully bent if necessary to achieve this.

Mark the position of the suction chamber and base and remove the damper by unscrewing the brass nut at the top and lifting it out. Then remove the retaining screws, after which the chamber can be lifted off, but be careful not to tilt it or you will bend the needle.

The piston assembly can now be lifted out, again very carefully without tilting, and the clevis pin and spring from the bottom of the jet can then be withdrawn from the bottom. Unscrew the jet adjusting nut and spring, followed by the

Fig. 12.12. A Stromberg diaphragm.

large jet locking nut, when the whole assembly can be removed.

This contains the spring-loaded glands that fit in the upper and lower jet bearings that allow the jet to slide up and down to enrich the mixture in place of a separate choke device.

The body casting is now bare, apart from the throttle assembly, which can be checked for excessive wear. If there is wear, new bushes (teflon-coated steel-backed) should be obtained and fitted. To do this the assembly is dismantled, the old bushes pressed out and the body line bored, preferably in a lathe or milling machine, to the appropriate size (8mm for the 1/4in spindle, 9.5mm for the 5/16in spindle) for the depth of the bush, not all the way into the venturi. The bushes are pressed in with a shouldered mandrel and new brass screws should be used when refitting the butterfly.

Replace the glands, washers, etc. with the new parts from the kit and rebuild the unit, leaving the jet adjusting nut loose at this stage. Ensure that the needle is straight and that its collar is flush with the bottom of the piston. Lightly oil the piston rod; the piston itself and the inside of the vacuum chamber must be clean (wipe with petrol or methylated spirits) and dry.

It is important that the needle is centred in the jet so that the piston falls with a definite clunk when the jet is pushed upwards as far as it will go. To achieve this the control linkage must be removed, the jet withdrawn together with the locking spring, and the adjusting nut replaced and fully tightened, and the large jet-locking nut loosened.

The piston damper is then removed and, with the piston rod pushed firmly down and with the jet held firmly against its adjusting nut, the locking nut is tightened. Check that the piston falls freely and reassemble the linkage. The hollow in the piston rod should be filled to just below the top with oil of SAE 20 grade and the damper replaced.

THE STROMBERG CARBURETTOR

As already mentioned, this type of carburettor is similar in principle and construction to the SU but the piston is controlled by a diaphragm and, unlike the SU, the needle is offset in the jet which is fixed. Mixture enrichment for starting is controlled by a disc valve.

Remove the carburettor in the usual way. The float chamber is released by undoing six holding screws and the float and needle valve taken out. The diaphragm and metering needle assembly is removed by first undoing the four screws holding the top cover assembly after removing the damper and draining the oil. The diaphragm is also held by four screws through a retaining ring which is removed, but release of the needle itself requires a special tool.

It is recommended by the manufacturers that the diaphragm is replaced every two years or 24,000 miles (40,000km) and it should be inspected very carefully for small cracks or bubbling. If it is renewed, be careful to fit it correctly; there is a lip on the underside which fits into a recess in the housing.

The needle valve and seating should be checked for wear, which is likely to show as ridging and grooving, in which case they should both be replaced. The metering needle should be straight and in good condition and should be replaced if there are any signs of wear. If the needle is worn or damaged it is quite likely that the orifice in the body has been affected, which is unfortunate as this will mean a new carburettor since spares are not available for either the top cover or air valve.

The throttle spindle should be checked for wear; the seals in the body are replaceable and are merely a push fit into their housings. Reassemble, clearing the orifices and passages by compressed air. The metering needle housing is refitted to the air valve with the special tool, screwing it in until the slot in the needle housing aligns with the grub screw, which should then be tightened into the slot so that the needle remains inclined under spring pressure towards the air cleaner side of the carburettor.

The float level is set, with the carburettor inverted, to a dimension of 0.625in to 0.672in (16mm to 17mm) measured from the top of the gasket to the top of the floats, making sure that they are equal by bending them if necessary, and that the tab bearing on the needle valve is positioned at right angles.

TUNING AND SYNCHRONISING

Having serviced the carburettor, its settings must be adjusted (tuned) so that it performs properly throughout the speed range of the engine. If there is more than one carburettor, it is necessary to ensure that all are operating in the same way by synchronising them.

The only really accurate way of doing this is to use a CO_2 meter, which measures the exhaust gas, and this is the method used by MoT stations when testing vehicles. CO_2 meters are available on the market but are probably not worth buying unless you propose to rebuild or maintain a number of vehicles; it is probably easier and cheaper to let the professionals do it for you. However, you can set the carburettors up very well to start with by following the normal procedure, which assumes that the ignition timing and tappet clearances are correct.

Warm the engine to its normal operating temperature, disconnect the linkages between carburettors and adjust the slow running screw(s) so that the engine is at tickover (about 700-800rpm for many engines but some running at about 1,000 rpm). The mixture screw in the case of constant choke carburettors (sometimes sealed), or the jet adjustment system of constant vacuum carburettors, are then very slowly adjusted in or out by small increments to give the maximum revs, readjusting the slow running screw as necessary if revs rise too high.

The smoke from the exhaust will tell you when the correct mixture has been obtained. This is when there is a regular and even note. An irregular note, with misfiring and a colourless exhaust indicates too weak a mixture, whereas a steady misfire and black smoke shows that the mixture is too rich.

With the constant vacuum carburettors, one test for the correct mixture setting is to lift the piston very slightly (about 1mm) using a small screwdriver. The correct setting will cause the engine to speed up slightly and then return to normal running. If the mixture is too rich, the speed will increase, and if too weak, it will decrease and the engine may stall.

These adjustments are made without the air cleaner fitted; a slight readjustment to weaken the mixture may be necessary when it has been connected.

Synchronising two or more carburettors follows after each has been tuned as far as possible and the settings of the idling screws are identical. The choke or other starting devices are disconnected and the linkages between the throttles slackened or disconnected, the air cleaner removed and the engine at normal working temperature. Each throttle idling screw is then adjusted so that there is no change in engine speed caused by either carburettor and the air flow into each is checked. Instruments are available for this purpose but a short length of tubing held against the inlets in turn will enable the hiss of the air being drawn into the choke tubes to be heard and compared, and the throttle butterflies adjusted so that the hiss is equal in each carburettor after which the linkage can be tightened. The slow-running screws can then be adjusted equally to give the required tickover speed.

AIR FILTERS

Before air is drawn into the carburettor or supply system of a fuel-injected system it passes through an air filter designed to remove, as far as possible, the abrasive dust with which air is laden in order to protect the engine from wear. In temperate climates with frequent damp weather this is not too big a problem, but in arid conditions the amount of airborne abrasive material can be very considerable.

Manufacturers have to balance the need to extract this material without restricting the air flow unduly, but after tuning an engine without its filter(s) it is sometimes necessary to weaken the mixture slightly.

For many years air filters have been replaceable items, changed at normal service intervals (though more frequently in dry climates). Sports cars tend to have small, individual filters of the 'pancake' variety (Fig. 12.13), largely to save space. These have elements made of woven steel wire which is cleaned by being washed in petrol. Depending on their type they may be lubricated by being dipped in oil after cleaning, and then drained, leaving an oily surface on the wire elements that holds unwanted dirt particles.

Earlier types were of the oil bath variety which worked in much the same way, though of a different shape, and some actually had a small quantity of engine oil in a small reservoir (hence oil bath). In many cases they were an integral part of a cylindrical container, sometimes very large, that formed an air silencer designed to subdue the hiss of air entering the carburettor.

FUEL INJECTION

The problem with a fuel system that incorporates carburettors is that it is impossible to ensure that each cylinder receives precisely the same quantity of fuel as the others, despite careful manifold design, and also because of the limitations imposed on air flow by the choke tube. It is for these reasons that sports and racing engines have used multiple carburettors –

Fig. 12.13. Twin 'pancake'-type air filters.

sometimes as many as one per cylinder – and why the twin-choke Weber instrument has proved so popular.

Fuel injection systems were designed to overcome these difficulties and to provide each cylinder with the precise amount of gas that it required in order to meet stringent emission requirements. At first they were mechanical with a series of pumps, one for each cylinder, spraying fuel into the inlet tract or directly into the cylinder in precisely metered quantities. These systems were eventually overtaken by extremely sophisticated (and reliable) electronic systems that take into account not only the driver's instructions but many other factors such as ambient temperature, air pressure, ignition timing, etc. to decide on the quantity of fuel to be injected.

If the project on which you are working was made after 1970 it may be equipped with this type of engine management system and the later the model the more complex it is likely to be. It will probably control not only the engine functions but also the alarm and accessories systems as well.

Some of the adjustment points both on carburettors and injection systems may be protected by tamper-proof seals or other fittings intended to prevent or at least discourage interference by those of us without the detailed knowledge and equipment to service them (and, getting it wrong, increase pollution). In some countries it is illegal to drive a car without the appropriate seals, though not in the UK.

Some cars are fitted with a fuel-pump inertia-switch which cuts off the power supply to the fuel pump (or closes a valve on cars with mechanical pumps) in the event of a collision or very sudden deceleration. If there is no fuel supply (check at the carburettor or fuel rail valve connection) reset the switch or valve before taking more drastic action.

DIESEL ENGINES

Compression ignition (CI) engines, as they are more properly called, have no carburettors or ignition system since they rely on the very high compression (about 16:1) in the cylinders to ignite the fuel. A fuel pump supplies diesel through a water trap and a filter to the fuel injection pump which in turn meters fuel to the injectors in the cylinders after the air inside them has been compressed, surplus fuel being returned to the tank.

Very little trouble is normally experienced with CI engines, and if you do have problems they are likely to be connected with the cleanliness of the fuel or wear in the injectors. Drain the water trap until neat fuel runs from it and check and replace the filter – the fuel system is made to such fine limits that almost microscopic particles can upset it.

If the engine misfires it is likely that one (or more) injectors is faulty: this can be identified by removing the feed pipe from the pump to each injector in turn. This will cause a marked drop in engine speed when the working injectors are disconnected but make no difference when the faulty one is disconnected.

Remember that the fuel is under considerable pressure, and direct the pipe away from you into a can to collect it. A test with a CO_2 meter will tell you if the injectors themselves are in good order; if not they are easily replaced. Anything more serious suggests that the pump itself needs replacement and you will then need the manual to follow the correct procedure for fitting and timing it.

Chapter 13

The exhaust system

The exhaust system is usually regarded as something of a necessary evil, and as it requires no maintenance and is normally hidden away under the vehicle it is forgotten about until things go wrong, when it is usually too late to do anything about it. If you are doing a total rebuild it is worth replacing the complete system, from the manifold onwards, unless there is evidence that it is in very good condition.

Replacement exhaust systems are available for almost every car built in the last 20 or more years from one of the tyre and exhaust specialists that exist in every town, and if a ready-made system is not available, they will make one up for you. If you do not possess a pit or a lift, a system is difficult to fit and it is best left to the specialists, since free fitting is normally part of the deal and you get the right fittings for it instead of having to bodge things up. There are also many firms offering systems in stainless steel which are inevitably more expensive at first cost but if you do a high mileage or are likely to keep the car for any length of time may be worth the extra outlay.

Exhaust manifolds are usually discoloured and may be pitted and rusty, which is a pity as they are often conspicuous when the bonnet is lifted. They can be cleaned-up by wire brushing and filing to get out the worst of the surface damage and sprayed with one of the varieties of very high temperature (VHT) paints that are obtainable, in a small range of colours, from accessory shops and direct from Frost Auto Restoration Techniques Ltd of Rochdale (www.frost.co.uk). The paint needs curing by heat if it is to remain very long and this can be done by running the engine as specified, but if you are not at a stage where you can run the engine, a domestic oven can be used as a partial substitute. Quality cars used to have their manifolds vitreous enamelled (like a non-plastic bath) which is very durable and good looking, though rather brittle and prone to chip if struck with anything hard.

Some sports cars have external exhausts which become something of a feature, especially on cars like the AC Cobra (see Fig. 13.1). These deserve chromium plating or, preferably, being made of stainless steel which can be polished, but a heat shield may be necessary to protect driver, passenger or admirers.

If you have a non-standard system, a local specialist will in all probability be able to make you a new system from separate parts, but may have to charge over the odds if there is a lot of cutting and welding. You can, of course, make your own using either parts from the local supplier or, if you want something special, from one of the performance catalogues. However, it is worth bearing in mind that the exhaust system on your car was designed to match the characteristics of the engine and that altering the system will not necessarily, by itself, give you more power, though it may give you more noise. The Demon Tweeks catalogue (www.demon-tweeks.co.uk), for instance, offers parts to make a complete system from the manifold flange itself onwards and includes pipes, bends, a variety of silencers and

Fig. 13.1. An external exhaust – one side of a Cobra with a V8 engine.

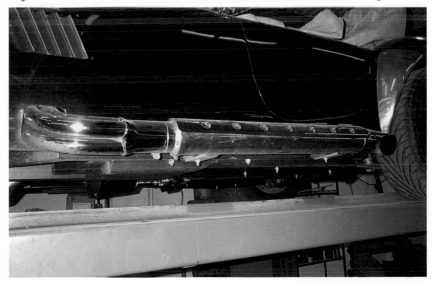

93

Fig. 13.2. Parts available to enable you to build your own system.

Fig. 13.3. Flexible exhaust pipe sections. Lengths of plain flexible tubing are also available.

shields (see Fig. 13.2). Though these are intended for performance enhancement they can be used to make up a standard system.

If you do make your own system it is very easy to let your enthusiasm get the better of you and finish up with an exhaust looking like a drainpipe which usually looks silly and amateurish. Depending on engine size it is rarely necessary to use an exhaust pipe of more than about 1 1/2in-1 3/4in though the tail pipe may be larger. If you make a new manifold with a four-into-one system, try to ensure that the lengths of the branch pipes are equal.

Keeping the exhaust from each cylinder separate for as long as possible helps to exhaust spent gas, as it minimises overlapping gas flow and so tends to improve performance by helping to reduce back pressure.

A modern exhaust system is suspended from the underside of the body or chassis by means of flexible hangers and is usually clamped solidly to the manifold so that it is free to move as the engine moves on its flexible mounting. If the system is a short 'side winder' type this freedom to flex is less easy to achieve and it is better to mount the silencer rigidly to the chassis/body structure and connect it to the manifold with a length of flexible exhaust tubing.

Fig. 13.4. Exhaust systems on transverse engines often have flexible joints of this pattern held together by springs.

Fig. 13.5. Exhaust pipe or drain pipe?

Chapter 14

Drivetrain

The drivetrain is the complete system that transmits engine power to the road wheels, and although differently disposed depending on where the engine is situated it contains the same elements.

We have already dealt with the clutch, so the next item is the gearbox. On cars with in-line engines this is a separate item bolted to the back of the engine behind the clutch, but on a transverse-engined car, such as the Mini, may be built into the sump and driven by gears from the crankshaft; on rear-engined or mid-engined cars with transverse engines it may be a separate unit.

In general, gearboxes give little trouble as they are enclosed and run in oil, and the best advice is to leave them alone if they are working. However, if you have reason to dismantle yours you should first drain the oil and wash it out with paraffin after the cover with its change mechanism has been removed. Many gearboxes have magnetic drain plugs that pick up small pieces of metal to prevent them floating about in the oil and damaging the working parts. Inspect this, and if there are any sizeable pieces inspect the gear teeth carefully to find out where they are from. If you had been able to drive the car you will know whether there were any problems such as noise or jumping out of gear, and of course any oil leaks will be apparent. If you were not able to drive the car, all you can do is inspect everything closely and try the shafts to see whether there is any play in them which would indicate worn bearings. Difficulty in engaging gears (if not attributable to the clutch) may be because the selector forks are bent. These may be made of an alloy and do not take kindly to brutal or ham-fisted treatment, so careful straightening is necessary. Jumping out of gear may be because of wear in the gears but is often caused by the spring-loaded balls in the selector mechanism not being strong enough to hold the gear in position; and the springs should be replaced.

Much more than this is not easily undertaken by the amateur, as gearbox overhaul on all but the most elementary boxes requires the use of special tools and gauges which only a specialist has, but the repair manual will normally cover the overhaul of the gearbox, so you can have a go if you feel like it. There are many specialists who will overhaul it for you, or if it is from a mass-produced car a visit to a breaker's yard may provide you with an alternative. Fig. 14.1 shows a typical four-speed synchromesh gearbox.

Fig. 14.1. A typical four speed synchromesh gearbox. (Austin)

95

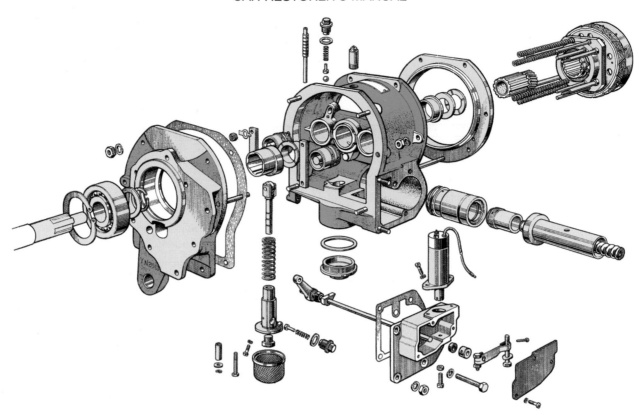

Fig. 14.2. An Austin Healey overdrive unit showing component parts. (Austin Motor Co.)

AUTOMATIC GEARBOXES

In general, automatic gearboxes are even more complex than the manual version and more difficult to overhaul as special equipment is needed to set them up. If there is a problem with gear changing, first check the fluid levels and the linkages before considering an overhaul.

GEAR CHANGE MECHANISMS

Gear change mechanisms vary from the gear lever that directly operates the selector forks, as on a Morgan, to the remote control variety. This also varies from the short lever of the sports car with a simple linkage to the selector forks to the more complicated systems required for transverse and rear- and mid-mounted engines, when the system becomes even more remote. It may consist of rods or cables, or a mixture of both, and

must allow for the flexible mounting of the gearbox. Rods have bushes that wear, and cables stretch, so careful adjustment of the mechanism and the replacement of any worn parts is essential for the optimum gear change.

Many cars of the '50s and '60s had the gear lever mounted on the steering column. Few of them made the act of changing gear a delight and some were quite horrid, resulting in a fight with the mechanism and a very leisurely change. All you can do is to put the system into the best possible condition and adjust – and lubricate – it carefully.

OVERDRIVE

Overdrive was a popular fitting on '50s–'70s sports cars, operating on top gear, and sometimes on second and third. Overdrive gave a fine selection of gear ratios and was instantly engaged by means of a switch on the gear lever knob or close to the steering wheel.

The unit consists of a single epicyclic train (see Fig. 14.2) which is held in engagement by oil pressure from its own pump and reservoir, actuated by means of a solenoid.

If you have problems, first check the oil level, and if this is in order, suspect the electrical system, which consists of a series of switches and relays that enable the unit to work when the appropriate gear is engaged. Check the fuse, and if in order try the action of the solenoid, bypassing the rest of the electrical circuit and connecting it directly to the battery. Replace this if faulty, and if not, go through the circuit carefully testing each item separately.

DRIVESHAFTS

Drive to the rear wheels is by means of a propeller shaft. If the rear suspension is not independent the whole axle moves up and down and provision has to be made for this movement, so the propeller

Fig. 14.3. A propellor shaft.

shaft is equipped with two, or if it is very long, three universal joints (UJs). As the length of the shaft also varies with the position of the axle a sliding joint is incorporated; this takes the form of splines in the output shaft of the gearbox mating with an extension to the first UJ (see Fig. 14.3). If you have occasion to take the shaft off the car, be sure to mark the flanges carefully so that you can replace it correctly.

Universal joints wear and can be tested by holding the shaft and twisting it by hand with a gear engaged. There should be no play in them. If there is, there will be a noisy clunk every time you change gear, and at other times when you use the throttle pedal.

Universal joints (on British cars often known as Hardy-Spicers from the name of the manufacturer) used to be equipped with grease nipples which were frequently neglected but later came packed with grease guaranteed for life (no one said whose).

Repair kits for some models are available (see Fig. 14.4 on the left) but in many cases the joint unit has to be replaced complete, though on some cars a complete replacement shaft may be required.

Shafts are balanced by the manufacturers and if damaged can set up unpleasant vibrations and also affect the ride quality, so it's worth inspecting them carefully. Long shafts are usually split in two with a central bearing on the chassis or underside of the body if a monocoque. This and its housing also need checking.

Cars with front-wheel drive, and rear-engined cars, have drive shafts which normally have constant velocity (CV) joints (see Fig. 14.4 on the right). These consist of three balls or rollers connecting two housings, the inner one driven and transmitting the torque to the outer and able to cope not only with the up-and-down movement of the suspension but also that required by the steering. The outer joints may need replacement – a clicking or knocking sound, especially on full lock, will indicate this. They are protected by rubber gaiters packed with a given quantity of grease; a split or leaking gaiter must be attended to as it will lose its lubricant and is in any case an instant MoT failure.

Some rear-drive cars have rubber 'doughnuts' instead of the more usual universal joints in their drive shafts, and the fact that specialist marque suppliers sometimes offer conversions to more normal UJs suggests that the rubber versions are capable of being improved upon either to give a longer life or better performance and are worth looking into.

Like the gearbox, the differential rarely gives trouble as it too is enclosed and runs in oil, but can be damaged through lack of oil or bad or competitive driving, and of course years of use can have their effect. This is especially true if a proprietary unit was used that was marginal in the first place, as in the early Morgan 4/4s where the rear axle was said to have been produced for a milk float! The result can be damaged gear teeth, wear on the teeth, especially on the large crown wheel and its driving pinion, and on the bearings. A constant whine when in motion will indicate that all is not well.

Earlier cars will have spiral bevel gears in their differentials, in which the pinion shaft lies on the same centre line as the half shafts, whereas later cars will have hypoid spiral bevel gears which are quieter and in which the pinion drive lies below the centre line of

Fig. 14.4. Left: A repair kit for a Hardy-Spicer type universal joint. Right: A typical constant velocity (CV) joint.

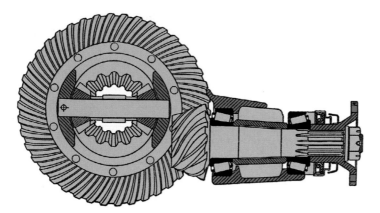

Fig. 14.5. A hypoid differential. Note that the pinion lies below the centre line.

Fig. 14.6. A worm drive. Some adjustment of this type is possible.

the differential, making a lower floor line possible (see Fig. 14.5).

Bevel gears are meshed correctly on production and cannot subsequently be satisfactorily readjusted for wear because the tooth profiles will have suffered and altering the mesh will only increase the amount of noise so that, as in the case of damaged gears, the only solution is replacement of the pair or unit complete. Worn bearings can be replaced, though again this may lead to increased noise if the new ones alter the mesh of the crown wheel and pinion materially. If you need to replace the crown wheel and pinion (and are fortunate enough to be able to find spares) instructions regarding mesh, backlash and pre-load of the pinion bearings will be given in the relevant workshop manual. The alternative, of course, is to obtain a replacement axle in better condition than your own.

Drain the oil from the differential housing and wash out with paraffin, rotating the gears by turning the propeller shaft or road wheels. If the contents drained out are not too frightening (broken teeth, metallic particles, etc.) and there are no undue noises, test for backlash. This is done by chocking the road wheels and turning the propeller or pinion shaft and checking the amount of free play which ideally should not exceed about 10°.

The star wheels in the differential unit which provide the differential action run on a two- or four-armed spider – depending on how many star wheels there are – the bearing surfaces of which can suffer through lack of lubrication, as can the inside of the star wheels. The spider arms can be built up by welding and then grinding to their original size and the bores of the star wheels bushed. It is surprising how much lost motion can be taken up by this means.

Oil leaking from the pinion bearing is one of the main causes of trouble and the oil seal should be renewed. If the pinion shaft on which the seal bears is worn it can be ground and an oversize seal fitted, but if this is not possible because it reduces the diameter of the splines it can be built up and reground to its original size.

A few cars – Peugeots and elderly Lanchesters and Daimlers – had worm drive instead of hypoid bevel; this was 'underslung' to lower the drive line and make a lower floor possible. Some adjustment of this type is possible, as shims in the worm shaft housing can be removed to compensate for wear in the tapered roller thrust bearings (see Fig. 14.6).

The back axle may be one of three types; semi-floating, three-quarter-floating or fully-floating, depending on how much load is placed on the half-shafts that drive

the wheels. The semi-floating type has a single roller bearing at its outer end on which the weight of the vehicle is supported and which also transmits the drive to the road wheels, leaving the end of the half-shaft on which the hub fits considerably overhung.

The three-quarter-floating type (Fig. 14.7) is similar but there is much less overhang as the bearing is placed on the centre line of the wheel. On the fully-floating type, normally found only on larger and more expensive cars, the half-shaft merely provides the drive to the wheels, the weight of the vehicle being taken on the ends of the axle casing on which the hub bearings are supported.

The inner races of the half-shafts are in the differential casing and are lubricated by the oil it contains, and on some axles this oil also lubricates the outer, wheel, bearings. Earlier cars often had a separate grease nipple to lubricate this race, which in the normal course of events was often neglected, so this bearing especially should be inspected and renewed if necessary.

To gain access, the road wheel is removed and the large nut on the end of the half-shaft, usually secured by a split pin, is removed. (Split pins should be removed by straightening their arms, clipping them off, and pulling out the remainder with a pair of side cutting pliers, tapping them out

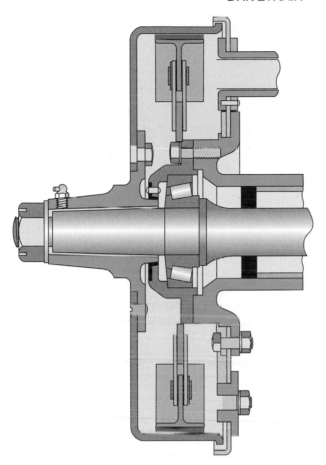

Fig. 14.7. A three-quarter floating type of back axle.

compressed air, giving it a coat of light lubricating oil to prevent it rusting, which it will very rapidly unless treated promptly. You can then spin it; if there is any play in it, or any gritty noise you will need a replacement. Take it with you to your bearing supplier who will read off the code from the small numbers stamped on it which will tell him the size.

It is worth taking the half-shaft out to examine the inner splined end. If the car has been used competitively or driven hard the shaft may be twisted and this is likely to show up where the splines emerge from the driving gears in the differential and especially at the outer, wheel end. If they are not exactly in line, the shaft should be changed. If the hub fits on a taper, remove it and try its fit on the taper without the key – it should be a firm fit, and if pressed on tightly should be solid with the shaft. If it is not, careful work with emery cloth and grinding paste on any high spots (which will be shiny) should restore the fit. You will, of course, have noted the condition of the oil seal and fitted a replacement if necessary.

Adjustment of the end-play of the half-shaft is effected by adding or subtracting shims between the flange on the end of the axle casing and the bearing housing. There should be no perceptible end-play, but the bearing must not be pinched up so tightly that it is not able to revolve freely.

If the axle is located by anything other than leaf springs you will need to look in detail at whatever arrangement is provided to locate and restrain it, but this is dealt with in Chapter 5.

When you have finished checking and overhauling the axle it should be painted like the chassis. Incidentally, if you have removed it from the vehicle you will find that it is a heavy and unwieldy lump. It is best placed on three axle stands, the third under the pinion shaft or nose of the differential casing, when it becomes much easier to work on.

with a parallel punch if necessary. Winding the nut off and shearing the pin is likely to damage the thread and make removal of the bit left inside more difficult.) The hub will be fitted to the shaft either on splines (in which case it should draw off easily) or on a taper with a key, when a puller may be necessary (Fig. 14.8).

The bearing housing can now be unbolted and the bearing removed, with or without its shaft. To clean a roller or ball bearing the best way is to degrease it, wash it under a jet of water and then dry it in a blast of

Fig. 14.8. A sectional view of one type of hub puller.

Chapter 15

Electrical system

WIRING

The wiring on older cars is often found to be in a sorry state, with poor earth connections (the cause of much electrical trouble) decaying insulation and, quite likely, overloading from additional equipment installed subsequent to manufacture. As such it is a source of many problems, the greatest of these being the very real risk of a potential fire.

If the wiring in your car is the old rubber-insulated sort, there's no option but to replace it entirely as the insulation will have hardened and started to crumble. Should you be anxious to retain the original look, it is still possible to obtain authentic-looking cotton braided wiring at not too much extra cost (see Fig. 15.1). The insulation underneath will be PVC, of course, but this won't show.

In the '60s, manufacturers began using PVC-coated wire, which they were able to colour-code in the same way as the braided coverings. Each major circuit would be allocated a plain colour, and wiring for it's sub-circuits would have a distinctive stripe (known as a tracer) added to the main circuit colour. There appears to have been no international agreement about which colour to use in which circuit, and although there was a British Standard not all manufacturers used it. However, the Lucas colour code was as follows:

BLACK	All earth connections
BLUE	Lighting switch to headlamps
BROWN	Main battery feed
GREEN	Accessories fused via ignition switch
LIGHT GREEN	Instrument voltage stabilizer to instruments
ORANGE	Wiper circuits
PINK/WHITE	Ballast terminal to ignition distributor
PURPLE	Accessories, fused, fed direct from battery
RED	Main feed to circuits supplied via sidelamp switch
SLATE	Window lift
WHITE	Ignition switch or starter solenoid to ballast resistor
YELLOW	Overdrive; fuel injection; central locking; gear selector switch to start

Cables also come in different thicknesses depending on the load they are required to carry and are referred to by the number of wires they contain and the diameter of each wire in millimetres. A 9/0.30 cable, therefore, consists of nine wires, each with a cross-section of 0.30mm. This is capable of carrying 5 amps, whereas a 14/0.30 cable (14x0.30mm wires) can manage 8 amps. These are the two most commonly used sizes, but the starter circuit and the charging circuit will

Fig. 15.1. A new wiring loom with cotton braiding.

have thicker cables. Depending on engine size, a starter motor may take anything up to about 300 amps while in use, consequently a much thicker cable is required to connect the starter solenoid (a relay) to the battery; 37/0.71 or 37/0.9 is commonly used. The generator, if a dynamo, may charge up to about 20 amps on a medium-sized car, whereas an alternator may double this. A cable of 65/0.30 should be used for a dynamo, and one of 97/0.30 for an alternator.

For many years PVC cables have been fitted with spade-shaped terminals (known in the UK as Lucar connectors) which are crimped onto the end of a cable and then pushed into place on an appropriate opposite-sex connector on the relevant electrical component. You may also find bullet connectors of both the solder-on and crimp-on variety. In earlier times, before crimping, terminals (ring or fork) were always soldered on to the cable and were secured by being bolted to the terminals on the unit (see Fig. 15.2).

Depending on the state of your wiring you can either replace it all, or merely replace those wires that are damaged. The best advice, though, is to fit a new system. Specialists, such as Auto Sparks of Nottingham (www.autosparks.co.uk), can supply wiring looms for most cars, with adaptations if necessary for different lighting arrangements (e.g. additional indicators).

If you are remaking your dashboard it is a good idea to cut the old loom off, leaving stubs of wire in place to act as a guide to what goes where.

If you are unable to buy a loom, or are determined to do your own thing, you will need reels of cable of the appropriate colours, and plenty of terminal fittings. It may not be economical to buy a reel of each colour/tracer combination and you may wish to use only the main colours without tracers. This simplifies things but makes tracing faults more difficult, and extra care in connecting up is required – it pays to label each terminal. You can either remove the original loom and replicate it, or wire directly on the car. If you do not have the loom you will have to work from the wiring diagram for your car which will be in the appropriate manual. These, especially on modern cars with many electrical accessories, are often difficult to follow and you will get on better if you spend some time with a pencil and paper and trace out each circuit separately, using crayons of the appropriate colour if you want to make things even easier. Rolls-Royce and Bentley for many years produced their wiring diagrams in colour (see Fig. 15.4 overleaf).

The size of the individual cables is important and should be the same as the original, or, if you intend to fit additional equipment, the next size up to cope with the increased electrical load. Too small a wire section creates a resistance, which as well as affecting the functioning of the equipment creates heat – and heat can lead to fire.

The sensible thing is to lay out the loom in the vehicle with reference to the original, and carefully remove each group of wires and replace it with the new ones, terminal for terminal and checking that all the grommets through which the cables pass are sound, replacing them as necessary. To help you pull the wires through holes, you may need a 'mouse' – a nail or similar on a length of cord, or a stretch of fairly stiff bare wire with a hook – galvanised garden wire is very suitable.

If you need more wires than originally provided, for additional circuits, now is the time to incorporate them, and if there is no spare provision in the fuse box, incorporate an in-line fuse holder in an accessible position.

Fig. 15.2. Soldered-on cable terminals connected by bolts to the back of this switch box.

Fig. 15.3. In-line fuses. The one on the left can be used on its own or clipped to others to build up a fuse box. The right-hand, tubular holder takes a glass fuse while that in the centre uses blade fuses but, as can be seen, you really do not need a holder at all.

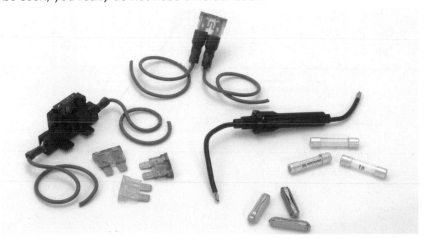

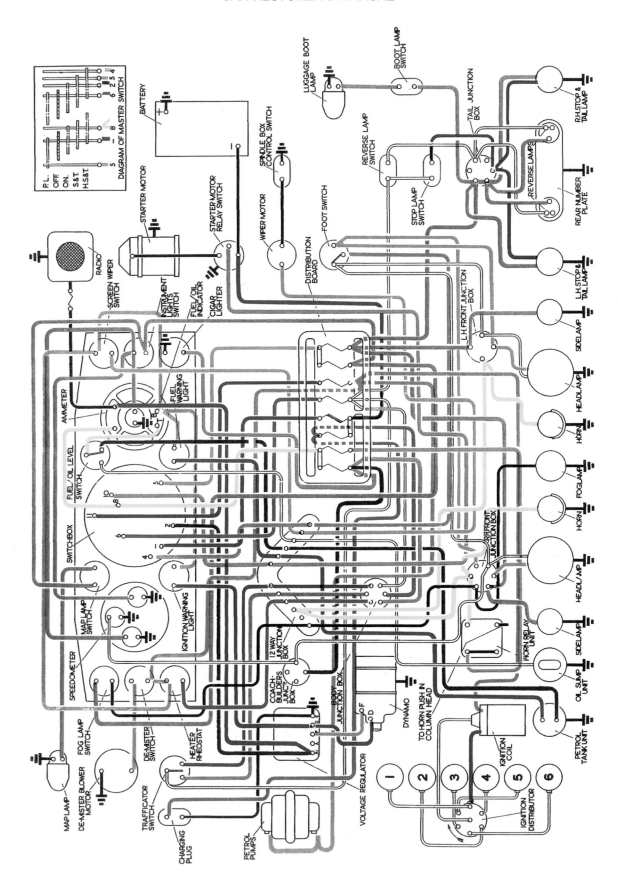

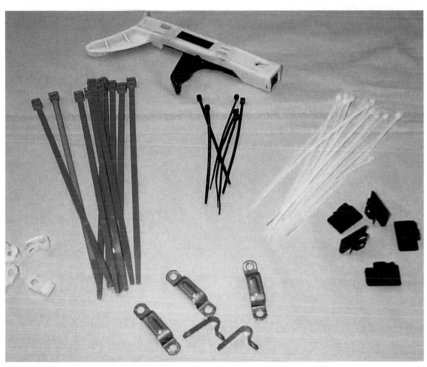

Fig. 15.5. Clips and ties for securing wiring.

All this should be done without the battery being connected and each circuit should be tested with a small meter as a precaution before connecting the battery for a final test. Replace all the fuses and, especially if they are of the glass or ceramic type, spend a little time in cleaning up their contacts as these often become corroded. A light spray with WD40 or similar will help to dissipate any moisture and keep them clean. Manufacturers seemed at one time to have had peculiar ideas about fuses, some having none at all and many only two for all of the circuits in the car (admittedly they were fewer as earlier cars had much less electrical equipment than modern ones). The more fuses there are the easier it is to trace the cause of blown ones. In line fuses (Fig. 15.3) are cheap and easy to fit and should be used for any additional circuits you install.

The cables in wiring looms are bound together with harness tape

Opposite: Fig. 15.4. A wiring diagram for a Bentley. (Bentley Motors (1931) Ltd)

(a non-adhesive PVC product that grips to itself) to provide strength and protection, as well as neatness, but there are other products, such as spiral binding, convoluted tube and flexible conduit, which can be used for extra protection. Expensive cars with exposed lamps and horns had wiring running through conduit or armoured sheathing which is impressive and virtually foolproof.

Be particularly careful over the connections you make to earth and ensure that the earth point does in fact connect to the rest of the car and is not in some way insulated from it. Coachbuilt bodies may be mounted on rubber or otherwise have no direct connection with the chassis, and engines and power trains always are. Connect these items to each other by means of earth straps – flat braided cables – otherwise you will be unable to complete some of the circuits, or you'll get intermittent electric problems. An effective earth strap is essential between the chassis and engine.

If your car has a glass fibre body, or if parts of it, such as the wings, are made of glass fibre, you will have to

ensure that the earth connections for the various units, such as lamps, go all the way back to the chassis or some common earth return, as glass fibre is itself a good insulator.

The wiring loom is secured to the car by means of clips and/or wiring ties (see Fig. 15.5). There are various types available from your local automobile electrical specialist, or direct by mail order from specialists such as Auto Sparks.

While you are doing the wiring it is worthwhile fitting a battery master switch. These are reasonably priced and, wired in to the main battery feed, will isolate it by means of a large, removable, key which is useful as a deterrent against car thieves and also is an easy way of disconnecting the battery when you are working on the car – some types have a built in fuse which allows some circuits, such as electric clock, central locking and alarm to remain operational with the rest switched off. Fit it in some easily-accessible but unobtrusive place if you can, as if it has to go under the bonnet natural laziness will mean that you are not likely to use it.

To cut down on the sheer mass of wiring, especially behind the dashboard, relays are commonly used. These are electrically-operated switches that can be placed close to the units they serve using only thin wires to their controls, and only short lengths of thicker wires to the units, such as head and fog lights, horns and other components that require a high current supply. Connections to them from the operating switch on the dashboard is by 9/0.30 and from them to their units by 14/0.30 or 28/0.30. Be careful when buying relays to get the type specific to the purpose as there are numerous types, each suited to a different function.

EQUIPMENT

The heart of a car's electrical system is the battery. Some modern batteries are sealed and never need topping up, in which

case (apart from ensuring that the terminals are in good order) you can fit them and forget them. But many types do need periodic checks on the level of the electrolyte, and topping up when necessary. The battery must be of the right size physically to fit into its space and be firmly clamped down to its carrier. The old carrier may need renewing, or at least a repaint after a good clean up with a wire brush as carrier bases are very prone to corrosion. If you can find a non-metallic battery tray for it to sit in this will protect the carrier from spilt electrolyte; if not, a piece of rubber matting is useful.

The battery must also be the right size electrically to cope with the loads imposed upon it by the equipment in the car. The load is particularly high when starting a large engine, or one with a high compression such as a sports car, and especially on a diesel engine, which not only has a very high compression ratio but also has to supply current to the heater plugs when starting. Cold weather also reduces quite markedly the amount of current a battery can supply just at a time when the engine is at its most reluctant because of reduced clearances and thicker oil.

The size of a battery is specified by the number of its ampere hours (Ah), that is for how many hours it will supply a current of one ampere (amp). For a small car, a battery with a capacity of 35Ah will be sufficient, for a medium-sized car 55Ah and a large one, or a diesel-engined car, 65Ah or more.

The battery is in effect a reservoir for storing electricity and needs constant charging to keep it full, as on a petrol-engined car there is a continual drain on it to supply current to the engine. It is charged by a generator which on older cars was a dynamo and on more modern ones, an alternator, the difference being that an alternator can be run at a higher speed than a dynamo and produces the greater current necessary for modern vehicles.

Fig. 15.6. A 12 volt dynamo.

DYNAMO

A dynamo consists of an armature, with coils of wire, that revolves inside a casing which also has coils of wire (field coils) wound on it. As it rotates a small electric charge is generated which is fed into the field coils, the generated current then very rapidly building up. Current from the rotating armature is collected by carbon brushes from the commutator, a series of copper strips connected to the armature coils. To work properly the coils must be in good condition, the commutator smooth and the brushes properly bedded-in, and of course the bearings must be satisfactory.

Fig. 15.6 shows a rather rusty 12 volt dynamo. To dismantle it you first need to remove the pulley retaining nut. If this is so tight that you cannot hold the pulley steady by hand, try locking the drive pulley with its belt using a Mole-grip wrench (see Fig. 15.7) or a vice. The pulley can then be removed with a gear puller (Fig. 15.8) if it is obstinate; it is keyed to its shaft and can sometimes be stubborn.

On this particular unit there was some shake in the bearing at the pulley end, so this was replaced after dismantling and cleaning was complete. Fig. 15.9 shows the main components.

Fig. 15.10 shows a commutator with the discolouration typical of much use, but otherwise in not bad condition. It could easily have been

Fig. 15.7. Undoing the pulley-securing nut.

Fig. 15.8. Removing a stubborn pulley.

Fig. 15.9. The main components of a dynamo – end casings, armature and field coils.

Fig. 15.10. An armature placed in a lathe so that the commutator can be skimmed.

Fig. 15.11. The commutator after skimming.

Fig. 15.12. Undercutting the commutator insulation.

Fig. 15.13. Brushes and brush holders.

brought up to a good state with a strip of fine sand paper (not emery cloth, as the abrasive particles tend to embed themselves and cause rapid wear of the bushes). However, the lathe was handy so a very light skim was taken off the commutator (Fig. 15.11). The very thin strips of insulation between the copper strips need undercutting slightly and while there are several ways of doing this, one of the easiest is to grind the 'set' off the teeth of a hacksaw blade and use it as in Fig. 15.12.

The field coils should be tested for continuity with the aid of a meter. With one meter probe at each end of the coil windings, if the needle does not give a reading, or it is very small, the windings of the coil have broken or there is a very high resistance. Carry out a similar test on the armature with the probes on adjacent segments. An insulation test should also be made on the armature by attaching one probe to the shaft and the other to each of the segments of the commutator in turn

– if a reading results there is a short circuit between the coil and earth. Now disconnect the field coils and attach one probe to one end of the field coils and the other to the casing when there should be no reading on the meter.

Check that the brushes are not damaged, and if worn down, replace them. The new ones will need bedding in to the contour of the commutator which is done by putting a strip of sand paper, abrasive side outwards, allowing the brushes to rest on it, and pulling it to and fro until the brushes make full contact.

A battery can be charged only with direct current (DC) and not alternating current (AC). Both dynamos and alternators produce alternating current, but the commutator-and-brush system of the dynamo acts as a rectifier changing the current to DC, whereas the alternator has to have a separate rectifier system.

Two controls are, however, necessary in a dynamo charging system – one to regulate the amount of current generated, the other to ensure that when the dynamo is not charging it is not being driven, like a motor, by the battery. Some very early cars had a switch on the dashboard which had to be operated manually to do

Fig. 15.14, The completed dynamo.

this, but as drivers forgot and returned to a car with a flat battery the electric switch or cut-out was introduced. This brings the dynamo into the charging system only when it is generating current.

The cut-out and regulator live in a little black box on the bulkhead and often incorporate the fuses as well. The regulator also operates like a switch, reducing the voltage to the field coils when the battery is fully charged, and only needs maintaining.

There are many different versions of these instruments, the settings of which can be adjusted, but as the values also depend on the type of dynamo and its output characteristics it is not possible to give them here. The workshop manual may provide the information. Alternatively, your automobile electrical specialist may still have the series of blue cards (see Fig. 15.19) that were issued by Lucas (the majority of British cars were fitted with Lucas equipment) giving the test procedures for its equipment and so be able to tell you how to proceed. All that is possible without this information is to ensure that the switch contacts are clean and in good condition. In general they give little trouble: if the charging rate of the battery is low, suspect first the adjustment of the driving belt and then the dynamo

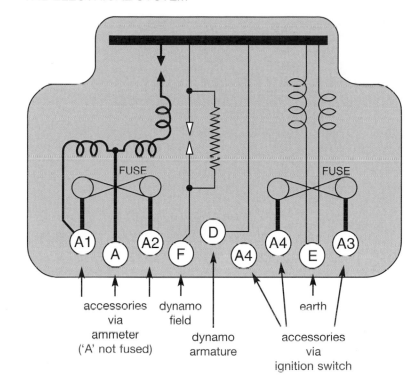

FUSE   FUSE

A1 A A2 F D A4 A4 E A3

accessories   dynamo
via   field
ammeter   earth
('A' not fused)   dynamo   accessories
                   armature   via
                              ignition switch

Fig. 15.15. Internal wiring of typical Lucas control box (Type RF95).

itself, but if the battery is being over-charged as shown by electrolyte bubbling out of the filling apertures, then the regulator is suspect. The wiring of a typical control box is shown in Fig. 15.15.

ALTERNATOR

The construction of an alternator is similar to the dynamo but it is

generally shorter and of greater diameter, the most obvious difference being that instead of a commutator there are two slip rings on which the brushes run. Check the condition of the bearings, slip rings and brushes, and replace as necessary. With a meter check the stator (field) coils for continuity – there should be three of them – one should be connected to the meter

Fig. 15.16. An alternator.

Fig. 15.17. The stator (field) windings. The diode pack is beneath the insulation.

Fig. 15.18. The slip rings on the end of the rotor (armature). The brushes are in the removable unit on the right.

Fig. 15.19. A collection of Lucas 'Service, Maintenance and Testing Procedures' pamphlets that covered most of their equipment. Similar information will be found in workshop manuals.

and the other probe used in turn on the other two, and then check the insulation, one probe to the coil and the other to the frame.

The rotor (armature) is tested for continuity and insulation in a similar manner, by connecting probes to each slip ring and then from one ring to the frame.

As already noted, the alternator produces alternating current (AC) which is no good for charging the battery and it has to be rectified to DC. This is done by diodes; early diode packs were a separate unit, but later ones are built into the alternator. The diodes are more likely to breakdown than the alternator itself and can be replaced, though it is worth checking the cost against a complete replacement unit, which, with guarantee, may be preferable.

Some early Lucas systems had a relay connecting the stator windings with the battery. The relay is housed, probably on the bulkhead, in an aluminium case and cannot be serviced. If the alternator appears to be in order but there is no charge to the battery, the relay is suspect and should be checked by a specialist, but ensure first that the connectors at the alternator are in good order and tight.

STARTER MOTOR

The starter motor is very similar in construction to the dynamo (see Fig. 15.20), though more robust, and works in the opposite sense in that it uses current rather than generating it.

The same tests used on the dynamo for continuity and insulation should be carried out on the starter, and the commutator dealt with similarly, except that the insulation separating the copper segments must not be undercut. Check the side play in the armature – if excessive, the bearings will need renewing.

Fig. 15.20. A typical inertia drive type starter motor.

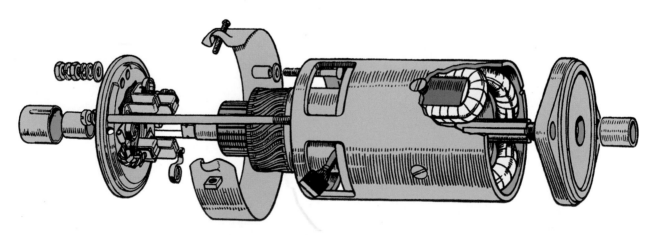

Fig. 15.21. The component parts of the inertia drive of a starter motor.

Later starter motors may have a face-type commutator rather than a drum type (see Fig. 15.22).

To check the system with the motor in place, first ensure that the battery is well charged; to check it, put the probes of a voltmeter to its terminals and with the ignition switched off, operate the starter. The reading should be 10.5 volts or above on a petrol engine, 10 volts for a diesel. If the battery is in good condition but the starter motor sluggish in operation then there is a high resistance in some part of the circuit. Test the connecting leads and the solenoid with a voltmeter to establish the cause of the voltage drop, and rectify accordingly. A low battery, or faulty solenoid, can cause the latter to chatter when attempting to start the engine.

In general, starter motors are very reliable, and troubles are more likely to be caused by a low battery, a poor solenoid, or a sticking Bendix drive on an inertia-operated system. The solenoid can be tested by removing one of the thick cables from the solenoid and touching it on the other, thus by-passing the unit. If the starter then operates, the solenoid is at fault and should be replaced.

If the starter revolves without engaging, or if it sticks in position and will not free itself, the trouble lies with the drive to the flywheel.

There are two main types of drive systems, the inertia and the pre-engaged. In the latter, the small pinion on the end of the armature shaft is meshed with the gear ring on the flywheel before the starter motor begins to revolve. On the more primitive (but once very common) inertia system the armature revolves first and causes the pinion to slide along its helical path and into engagement with the

flywheel ring (inertia stops it revolving with the armature) when it reaches the end of its travel and is forced to revolve. When the engine starts and the flywheel speed is greater than that of the

Fig. 15.22. A face-type commutator (instead of a drum-type) used in many starter motors.

Fig. 15.23. Splines on an starter armature shaft on which the screwed sleeve slides.

pinion, the pinion is spun back along its track where its impact is absorbed by a heavy spring.

This mechanism, usually known as the Bendix drive (see Fig. 15.21) is not normally lubricated, and if worn or the spring is broken it must be replaced. It is normally replaceable as a unit as it is mounted on splines on the armature shaft (see Fig. 15.23), and at one time small dedicated spring compressors were available to

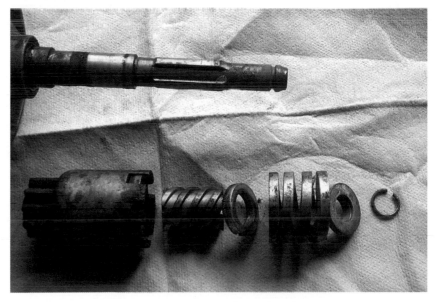

Fig. 15.24. An inertia drive spring compressor.

Fig. 15.25. An inertia drive in pieces. (Peter and John Wallage)

enable it to be taken apart (see Figs. 15.24 and 15.25). At the other end, accessible without dismantling, but originally under a small cap, the squared end of the armature protrudes so that it may be turned with a spanner to unwind the pinion if it gets stuck in the flywheel.

If trouble persists, despite rectification of the drive, it is likely to be caused by wear on the flywheel ring gear teeth and action should be taken as detailed in Chapter 10.

Troubles with pre-engaged starter engagement mechanisms are rare, often restricted to the contacts of the solenoid, but these systems embody a clutch in the drive, which operates when driving the pinion and is freed when the ring gear starts to revolve. These clutches are usually roller driven and are replaceable. Some modern starters have permanent magnets instead of field coils and are geared down; Rolls-Royce starters are geared down and also have plate clutches to prevent damage in case of a backfire.

IGNITION SYSTEMS

For many years petrol-engined cars have had an ignition system consisting of a coil and distributor unit which includes a contact breaker.

As far as the coil is concerned there is little you can do about it. It is sealed for life and it either works or it does not. Some systems, however, use a ballast resistor (see Fig. 15.26) and work on a lower voltage (8 or 9 volts) to help the performance of the coil under starting load, so this resistor needs checking as well if the coil's performance seems substandard.

The high tension leads from coil to distributor and from distributor to plugs are worth attention to ensure they are at least clean and dry and preferably not bundled together but supported and kept apart by insulated separators to prevent the spark from one lead tracking to another or to earth. Early carbon resistor leads, which are wire less, as fitted to cars of '70s vintage are often a problem. They can break down intermittently, giving all the

Fig. 15.26. A typical ballast resistor.

symptoms of misfiring, and are best replaced with modern silicone HT leads with built-in suppression or the ordinary wire type with suppressed plug caps.

DISTRIBUTOR

This unit is the weakest link in the engine's electrical system, if not the car, and consequently requires proper setting up and maintenance. It contains the contact points that cause the coil to provide the spark for the sparking plug; the distributor to switch the sparks to the correct cylinder, and two quite separate systems to adjust the timing to the speed and load of the engine.

Before removing it from the engine, note the position of the distributor body, or if it is held on by a clamp with only one bolt, mark the body and the clamp so that they can be reassembled in the same relative position – also note the position of the rotor arm. Remove the unit from the engine and, after cleaning externally, take off the cap and leads and the rotor arm. Clamp the body gently in a vice and check the bearings for side play. If any exists it will result in erratic running as the timing and contact breaker gap will be affected. Check also inside the cap to see how the rotor arm contacts are worn; unequal wear suggests play in the shaft. If there is play,

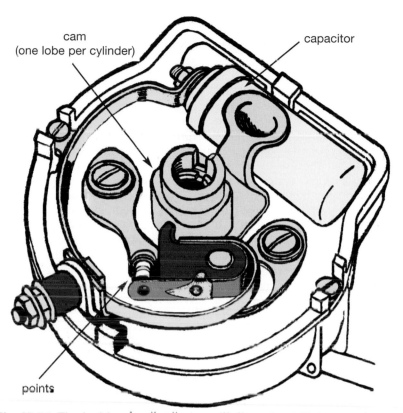

cam
(one lobe per cylinder)

capacitor

points

Fig. 15.27. The inside of a distributor with the rotor arm removed.

you may be able to fix it with a replacement bush kit, but if one is not available try your local bearing supplier or have some turned up.

The shaft assembly can be removed by taking off the drive gear or dog, usually held by a pin which should be tapped out, and with the contact-breaker plate taken off, the bushes can be removed in the usual way. Clean the balance weight pivots and lightly lubricate them with oil, and check that the springs have not been distorted – they are carefully chosen to suit the characteristics of the engine, the performance of which will be adversely affected if they are incorrect or not in good condition.

The cam should be shiny and without wear; much depends on this and if you need to replace it (or the complete distributor unit) ensure that it is from the same model. The plate that holds the contact-breaker should be cleaned and the post holding the breaker

lightly lubricated. The points on the breaker need to be clean, without pitting or piling – you might as well start off with new ones. The plate should be free to move about a small arc – it is connected to a vacuum-advance unit (a diaphragm) which is spring-loaded so that it should return to its

original position when released. The diaphragm is connected to the induction manifold by a small-bore plastic pipe with rubber connectors at each end (see Fig. 15.28). These perish and break in time and should be replaced – the accessory shop will sell you new ones. Earlier cars may have a centrifugal advance rather than a vacuum unit.

Put a smear of light grease on the cam, otherwise you may get a continual squeak from it, and adjust the breaker points with a feeler gauge to the specified gap. Treat yourself to a new rotor arm and distributor cap and re-fit the plug leads in the same order as originally fitted – it is a good plan to mark the plug leads so that you can easily refit them to the correct cylinder, especially on six- or eight-cylindered engines. Neat little sleeves with numbers are available for this purpose or you can file notches on the plug caps.

When refitting the unit to the engine it is necessary to time it so that the sparks happen at exactly the right time in the cycle of events. If the distributor has a drive dog at the end of the shaft the protruding tongue will probably be off-centre so that it will fit in only one position, and provided you bolt the distributor back in its original position you need do no more. If the tongue on the dog is not asymmetric you have the choice of two positions, at 180°, and

Fig. 15.28. Piping for connecting the automatic advance diaphragm to the inlet manifold.

the note you made as to which cylinder the rotor arm was pointing will enable you to make the correct decision, providing of course that the engine has not been turned in the meantime. If it has, or instead of a dog there is a gear on the end of the shaft, turn the engine until No.1 cylinder (nearly always the one nearest to the timing case or camshaft drive) is at top dead centre on the firing stroke (that is, it has both valves closed and the piston at the top of its travel) and replace the distributor so that the contact breaker points are just about to open. Rotation of the shaft may be clockwise or anti-clockwise, so make sure that the points are opening and not closing. The contact in the distributor cap nearest to the rotor arm will be for number one cylinder; the other plug leads should be connected according to the firing order of the engine which if not given on the engine itself, will be in the handbook or manual, or you can ascertain by noting the sequence of the valve events when turning the engine – TDC on firing stroke, plug lead to appropriate contact in the cap.

This ignition system served well-enough for many years, but as engines began to work at higher speed and compression ratios also rose, its shortcomings became more apparent. Manufacturers began to replace the contact breaker system with magnetic or optical systems, or with a transistorised system which retained the contact breaker only as a switch. Other methods were developed, including various forms of capacitor discharge systems, some of which have transformers instead of coils (but which look like the ordinary coil just to confuse us), before the introduction of the microprocessor and the disappearance of the distributor altogether.

Aftermarket kits were available, such as Lumenition and Mobelec to improve the performance of the ordinary distributor system, and some are still available if you look

at the advertisements in the enthusiast motoring press.

TESTING THE SYSTEM

The basic test of the system is whether it works or not, but if it does not the reason why is not always obvious. There are methods of ensuring that it is performing properly under all conditions, but these tests do not apply to electronic systems (they may be damaged by them).

The coil can be tested by removing the lead from the coil and holding it (with insulated pliers!) about 1/4in (6mm) from an earth point. Turn the engine with the ignition on and healthy sparks should appear. If not, check with a voltmeter that there is battery voltage at the SW (switch) terminal of the coil by connecting the voltmeter's red lead to earth and black to the SW terminal. With the ignition on, and the contact breaker points closed, there should be full battery voltage (or about half for a ballasted system). If this is satisfactory, the coil or capacitor (condenser) in or at the distributor is faulty. Substituting the capacitor for a new one will show whether the original capacitor was at fault, or the coil.

The ballast resistor, if fitted, is tested by temporarily wiring from the negative on a negative-earth system terminal to earth and measuring the voltage at the positive terminal. Cranking the engine should show a rise in the voltmeter reading. If not, check the lead from the coil to the solenoid ignition terminal. If this is in order, change the resistor.

If there is no spark at the contact breaker points when flicked open, the capacitor may be at fault, but if you have had the unit in pieces, check that you assembled the contact breaker correctly, and that it and its short connecting lead are both insulated from earth.

The distributor cap may have a hairline crack in it which shows itself by misfiring or poor starting.

Trying a substitute cap is the only way of checking it.

TESTING AND SETTING

The contact breaker gap is normally set by using a feeler gauge of the appropriate value (probably 0.014 to 0.016in or 0.35 to 0.40mm). A more accurate way is to use a dwell angle meter. The dwell angle is the period, measured in degrees, that the points remain closed during the rotation of the cam. With the points set too close together the dwell angle is increased and retards the ignition, too wide and the dwell is reduced, advancing the ignition. With the engine running, a dwell angle meter measures the actual angle, and therefore the points gap, and is the most accurate way of setting them. If you have a meter that measures the dwell angle, the accompanying literature will give you the actual values for most popular cars, but 54° is common for four-cylinder engines and 36° for six cylinders.

Start by setting the points with a feeler gauge and then check with the meter, being careful to set it for the number of cylinders of the engine being tested, and if the reading is not as specified, adjust the points as necessary. On most cars this means stopping the engine to make the adjustment, but on some distributors (notably Marelli) the manufacturers designed things so that the adjustment can be made with the engine running, by means of an insulated Allen key.

The other test is of the operation of the automatic advance and retard mechanism, which requires a stroboscope. This is an intense, bright light which flashes very briefly when activated. It is used in conjunction with the timing marks usually found on the crankshaft pulley or on the flywheel, in the latter case visible through an aperture in the casing. Identify the appropriate mark, if there are more than one, and paint it white or put chalk on it so that it is easily picked out. The strobe is connected to the number one plug lead; the distributor clamp slackened slightly so that it can be rotated by hand; the vacuum advance pipe removed; the manifold orifice blocked and the engine started and allowed to tick over. The strobe lights briefly when the plug fires and when directed at the timing mark appears to make this stationary, so it's possible to see whether it lines up with the fixed mark. The distributor has to be adjusted until it does.

Speeding up the engine should cause the timing mark to move backwards, against the direction of rotation, showing that the ignition is being advanced as the speed increases. When all is well the distributor clamp is tightened and the vacuum connection restored.

FUEL PUMPS

Cars of the period we are dealing with are likely to have either electric or mechanical pumps to supply the carburettor(s) with fuel. The most common electric pump was the SU (see Fig. 15.29) which consists of a diaphragm which pulsates under the action of a solenoid, alternately sucking petrol into a small chamber on one stroke and expelling it on the next, the action being controlled by valves.

This was often installed on the bulkhead and could be heard ticking, especially when priming the carburettor – no tick, no fuel supply. The then remedy was to tap it, when it would usually start ticking again, but inevitably there came a time when some maintenance was necessary. In fact, it is a most reliable component and requires little attention other than to the points.

A spring acting on the diaphragm forces petrol through the non-return outlet valve to the carburettor when this requires topping up. The diaphragm is then returned to its original position,

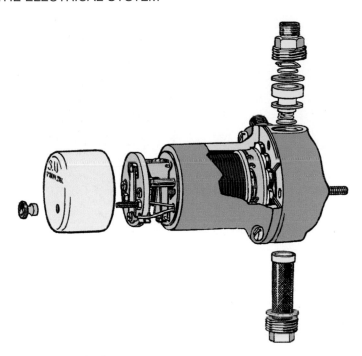

Fig. 15.29. An SU fuel pump.

sucking in petrol from the fuel tank through the non-return inlet valve as it does so, by magnetism created by a coil of wire surrounding an armature to which the diaphragm is secured. The timing of this is controlled by a pair, or sometimes two pairs, of contacts which remain open throughout the inward stroke and closed on the output stroke, and operate through a rocking lever mechanism.

At rest, the contact points should be touching each other and should be cleaned by passing a thin piece of card between them. When open, there should be a gap of about 0.03in. If they remain open or if the pump still fails to operate, remove the screws holding the cover of the suction chamber, take off the cover and dismantle the pump. The diaphragm should be in good condition and not be stuck to the end cover. Replacement parts, including diaphragms, are available from Burlen Fuel Systems Ltd (www.burlen.co.uk).

When refitting a diaphragm you will need to follow the proper procedure in order to set the rocker points correctly.

1. *Assemble the rocker mechanism in the pedestal and tighten the two retaining screws holding it to the pump body, but do not fit the contact blade at this point.*

2. *With the spring in position behind the diaphragm, screw the diaphragm rod into the barrel nut in the rocker assembly until it emerges from the other side. Continue screwing it in slowly, repeatedly pressing it against the spring until the rocker assembly throws over. Stop screwing the rod in at the exact point where the throw over action ceases.*

3. *Unscrew the diaphragm to the point where the six holes line up with the six holes in the pump body and then unscrew it by four more holes, i.e. two-thirds of a revolution. The diaphragm and rocker assembly are now correctly set.*

If the pump operates but fails to deliver fuel, check and clean the gauze filter at the bottom of the chamber, and unscrew and prise out and clean the seating of the two valves, which may be in the delivery chamber or in the base of the pipe connections. When

Fig. 15.30. A dual SU fuel pump removed for rebuilding.

pumps side by side which are sometimes switchable. Note that some pumps are designed to suck rather than deliver; these are placed on the bulkhead whereas those designed for the opposite function will be found close to the tank.

Fig. 15.30 shows a pump with two solenoids and a common chamber as removed from the car ready for rebuilding. Fig. 15.31 shows the rocking mechanism in situ and Fig. 15.32 with it removed from the pump, together with the blade contacts, both sets of which were cleaned up on a small, fine oil stone. One diaphragm is shown in Fig. 15.33 together with the valves in the chamber with their retaining plate, and without it in Fig. 15.34. The diaphragms were replaced as

replacing the pump, or refitting it, ensure that the valves are at the top and the filter at the bottom.

Some cars with large engines use two pumps with a common chamber; others may have two

Fig. 15.31. Removing the terminal post from the rocking mechanism plate. (Peter and John Wallage)

Fig. 15.32. The mechanism removed from the pump, showing the double contact points. (Peter and John Wallage)

Fig. 15.33. Diaphragm and valve chamber.

Fig. 15.34. The valves.

Fig. 15.35 The pump ready for refitting.

a matter of course, one new end cap was necessary and both solenoids assembled to the chamber with new gaskets, while the outsides were painted and new band seals fitted (see Fig. 15.35).

On cars fitted with fuel injection systems a fuel pump of different design is fitted. This is a small electric motor with a rotary pump built in which supplies a pressure-regulated system and is often fitted in the tank itself or very close to it. It is not normally capable of being serviced and should be replaced if faulty.

ELECTRIC MOTORS

Various other electric motors are fitted to cars to operate such equipment as windscreen wipers, window lifts, etc. Many are sealed and can only be replaced, but before you order a replacement unit check that the fuse and wiring to the malfunctioning motor is intact and that there is current at the terminals. It may be possible to dismantle some of the earlier types, though, following the procedure outlined above for the dynamo and starter. If the car has been unused for any length of time, often all that is required is a good clean and replacement of old oil or grease on the bearings, together with attention to the brushes and commutator.

DIRECTION INDICATORS

The current type of flashing direction indicators came into use in the '50s and replaced the previous semaphore type (often referred to as trafficators). The semaphore type (still available from specialists) consists of a metal-framed plastic arm which is lifted out of its casing in the bodywork by means of a solenoid operating through levers and lighting up a festoon-type bulb when fully raised, returning to its housing under its own weight when the current is switched off. On British cars, original equipment was usually of Lucas manufacture, though other manufacturers produced similar designs.

Access to the bulb is by removing the yellow plastic arm. A screw at its tip allows the metal plate supporting the plastic to be lifted away revealing the bulb and its spring lead (see Fig. 15.36).

The usual troubles with this type of indicator are a lack of lubrication on the pivots (which need oiling sparingly with thin oil); or over-lubrication which overflowed onto the plunger and dried out, causing it to stick; or through an electrical fault. Check that there is current at the terminal when switched on and test the solenoid for continuity. The arm drops onto a rubber buffer which if not properly positioned can lock the arm.

Spares are available for some types of these trafficators and it is as well to put them back into working order, though as they are not so obvious to other road users it's a good plan to fit the modern flashing type as well.

HEADLIGHTS

It took manufacturers a long time to come to terms with the challenge of dipping headlights to prevent dazzling oncoming drivers, and the simple solution of a twin-filament bulb did not come into general use for many years. Before this, some cars used the Barker dipping system which consisted of a lever, like an old-fashioned handbrake lever, connected by rods to the headlights, which were pivoted and literally dipped together when the driver operated the lever.

A later and much more widely used system was that known as the dip and switch system in which, when the dip switch was operated, the outer headlight was extinguished completely and the nearside was dipped by means of a solenoid operating a pivoted reflector. Other systems switched out both headlights and switched on a single driving light, centrally mounted.

Even if now legal, none of these systems is adequate for night driving in modern conditions and it makes good sense to adapt your lights to take more modern bulbs and systems, but do not be too rash with the power (wattage) of the bulbs because the dynamo output is likely to be limited and with the other demands made of it, such as rear and side lights and ignition, there will not be too much to spare.

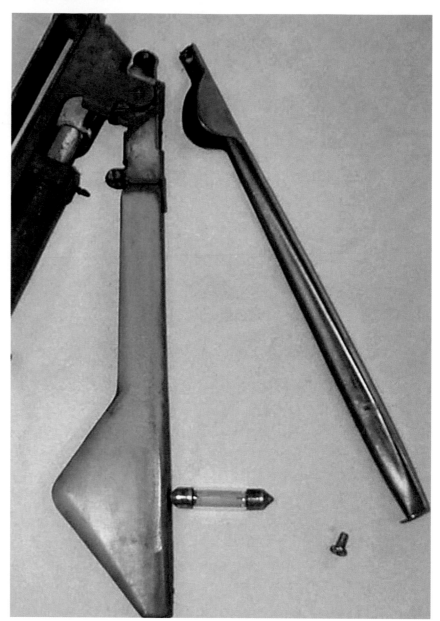

Fig. 15.36. A 'trafficator' – replacing the festoon bulb.

Chapter 16

Painting

This is one of the most exciting parts of the restoration, but it is time consuming and, if you have it done professionally, expensive. If you intend to do it yourself you will need paint spraying equipment, which you can buy or hire from a local tool hire shop. But it's possible you don't need a respray at all, or at most only a partial one. If the paintwork has dulled over it may be possible to resurrect it, touching in only the areas that need it. Neglected paintwork eventually dulls, and sunlight can affect it (red paint especially is prone to dulling and fading if subject to prolonged sunshine).

First wash the car thoroughly and then, using 1200 wet and-dry abrasive paper, rub it down. The rubbing-down process requires plenty of water, so you need to do it outside. Requirements are a bucket of water, a sponge, some bar soap, a rubbing down block made of rubber and a pair of industrial rubber gloves. The abrasive paper is attached to the block and thoroughly wetted and wiped on the soap so that the abrasive does not become impregnated with paint particles. The area on which you are working is wetted with the sponge, and the rubbing block with paper attached rubbed evenly over the surface until there is an even satin finish. The block must be washed frequently in the bucket and the working area kept wet while you are working. When the whole car is finished, wash it again to remove any paint or abrasive debris and then burnish it. Burnishing is done with a rubbing compound or a

liquid such as T Cut, and it must be applied on a clean cloth, frequently turned as it becomes impregnated with dead paint. As you rub, the paint will begin to shine, and as soon as the compound dries white, wipe it off with a clean cloth. An application of car polish will help to seal in the shine and you may have saved yourself a lot of work or expense in not having to respray the car.

It is worth noting that this method will not work on modern finishes known as clear-over-base, as the pigmented paint is first sprayed on and then covered with a clear coat which gives the shine, but such finishes are much less prone to fading so that remedial treatment should not be necessary anyway.

Fig. 16.1. Red paint is prone to fade.

If the paint is too badly damaged for this treatment or you have fitted new panels or otherwise repaired the bodywork, this will not work and you will have to refinish either the complete car or separate areas. If the latter, it is usual to respray a complete panel whenever possible, but touching in of small areas is also possible.

Paint has an identifying code and it is usually found on a small plate either under the bonnet or in the boot. When you buy paint you will need to quote this number to the supplier – the fact that you have a red Ford of a certain year may not be terribly helpful (when I was respraying a Triumph Stag I discovered that no fewer than four completely different shades of red had been used in the same year)

117

Fig. 16.2. The author's Triumph Stag after respray, awaiting application of black stripe on the front wing.

PREPARATION

If you have not already done so, strip the car of as many fittings as possible, including window glass if you are doing a complete re-paint, and mask off anything that you do not remove but do not want painted. Use good quality masking tape, not the thin cheap stuff available for home decorating, and proper masking paper from the supplier if at all possible. Newspaper was at one time freely used but as it now may contain silicon – which is the enemy of all good painting – it is wise to use the proper stuff. During the course of the painting process much water will be used, so do not stint on the masking and cover all areas that may be subject to overspray as well as those directly involved.

Most decorative finishes depend for their success on good preparation and this is most certainly the case when painting a car. Ideally you will have garage accommodation which is warm, dry, well-lit and well-ventilated with space to walk freely round the car, as well as room outside so that you can push the car out for the rubbing down operations which involve copious supplies of water.

Before you start to paint you must ensure that the panels, or complete car, are ready to receive the paint. If repairs have been undertaken, or there are any blemishes, these must first be prepared. Corrosion and damage will have been repaired when you were working on the body, but there are likely to be dents, scrapes and other minor indentations that need to be filled to bring about a completely flat surface to receive the paint which would otherwise only highlight the damage.

Common practice is to use a two-part resin filler, and this will work equally well on steel, aluminium and glass fibre bodies. There are various types on the market but they all work in the same way. Mix an appropriate amount of paste and catalyst

and there are innumerable shades of black. If you are only spraying a panel or other limited area a problem arises, especially if the car is old, as the original finish may have changed colour slightly and any new paint will be different. The professionals go to great lengths to match the new to the old, and if you take a piece of the car, such as a flap from the petrol filler cap, the supplier may be able to mix an exact match, but they will need to start with the colour code.

Depending on the state of the paintwork you will have to decide whether to respray the whole car or merely a part of it and also whether to strip it back to bare metal or merely spray over the existing finish when it has been prepared. A bare-metal respray will be more expensive and time consuming but more satisfactory as it will not be subject to any possible adverse affects caused by the old paint underneath. It can, nevertheless, be quite satisfactory to spray on top of existing paint if this is properly prepared, and if the car is not especially valuable it may not warrant the considerable extra expense involved in stripping off all the old paint and starting from bare metal.

The later stages of applying paint are the same but the preparation necessary will depend

on whether you are removing all the old paint or not, and whether the bodywork is pressed steel, aluminium or glass fibre, but a word first about the equipment you will need for spraying.

This consists of a source of compressed air and a spray gun matched to it. Compressors come in a wide variety of sizes. They normally consist of an electric motor driving an air pump mounted on an air receiver which stores the compressed air enabling sudden demands to be made on it and smoothing out the air flow from the pump. They are usually fitted with a water separator, as air contains moisture which is detrimental to paint spraying. The compressor should be able to produce a pressure of about 60psi (most will produce 100psi plus) and an output of free air of about 4-5 cubic feet per minute, which most small units, if equipped with a receiver of 25 litres or more capacity, can manage. They will have an electric motor of about 11/2hp and can be operated from a normal 13 amp supply.

The spray gun should preferably have controls for air and paint delivery and a nozzle that is not too large for the air supply; if in doubt it is better to err on the small side and go for a nozzle of 1mm diameter.

together in the proportions given by the makers and spread the filler onto the area of bodywork in need of treatment with a clean plastic or steel spatula. Leave the surface proud so that when it's set you can flat off and smooth it with a rubbing block and wet-and-dry paper. Normally, the filler will set in about 15 to 20 minutes, but too much catalyst will accelerate the process. It is better to underestimate the quantity of filler required and add another layer than overestimate it and be left with a surplus that will go off (harden) before you can use it.

The more traditional and professional way of filling is lead loading, a process by which lead (actually plumber's metal, which is a form of solder) is melted onto the surface of the defect. This method is much used on better quality cars for filling both indentations and seams.

The sequence of photographs (Figs. 16.6 to 16.11) shows how lead loading is done. First, the area to be filled is cleaned and brought up to a bright state by using an angle

Figs. 16.3 and 16.4. Resin filler flatted off.

Fig. 16.5. A respray over existing paint, after proper preparation.

Fig. 16.6. Preparing the surface before leading.

Fig. 16.7. Clean and bright, ready for tinning.

Fig. 16.8. Tinning the area, using solder paint.

Fig. 16.9. Heating with a soft flame.

grinder. Fig. 16.7 shows what it should look like. Next, before the solder can be applied it is necessary to 'tin' the area, and Fig. 16.8 shows this being done by brushing on solder paint (a mix of powdered solder and flux). The area must then be heated. In Fig. 16.9 an oxyacetylene torch with a soft flame is being used, but an amateur would probably be better off using an ordinary gas blowlamp to avoid overheating the work. Now is the time to apply the 'lead'. With the aid of a flame, dab it onto the preheated area in small lumps as soon as it melts, rather than trying to make it run (see Fig. 16.10). A spatula must now be used to smooth the lead into the depressed area and to bring it to the required level (Fig. 16.11). Keep

the spatula oiled or greased to prevent it sticking. A very good finish can be achieved by this method, and final finishing can be done with abrasive papers or by filing.

PAINT

The two-pack and clear-over-base paints used in the trade are largely out of bounds for home use because some of them contain cyanide and other unpleasant substances, and they can only be used in purpose-built booths equipped with special compressor-fed breathing apparatus. Also, a high level of skill is required to achieve a good finish. The amateur's best choice is traditional cellulose-based paint, since no

special precautions are required for its use (though it is toxic and flammable) and, with scope allowed to rectify mistakes, an excellent finish is possible – though it may take some hard work to achieve it. For safety's sake wear a mask when spraying, and if possible leave the workshop doors open to allow fumes to clear quickly. Make sure there are no naked flames, and store your paint and thinners away from heat.

On pressed-steel bodies, having done all the preparation work, the first coats of primer/filler can now be applied, but first wipe the bodywork with a cloth dampened with panel wipe, or with a tack cloth, to remove dust and other impurities. The paint will need to be thinned as it will be far too thick to be sprayed straight from the tin. Try a 50:50 proportion of paint and thinners to start with and adjust it as necessary. A double pass with the spray gun followed by a pause of about 20-30 minutes to let the solvents flash off before repeating the spraying will gradually build up the paint until, after three or four applications, you have a solid deposit.

When dry, the paint must be flatted-off with grade 320 abrasive paper which will show up any high or low spots. The low areas can be filled, and any high spots may be rubbed down if in the paint, but if they stand too proud the panel will

Fig. 16.10. Applying the metal.

Fig. 16.11. Smoothing the molten metal with a spatula.

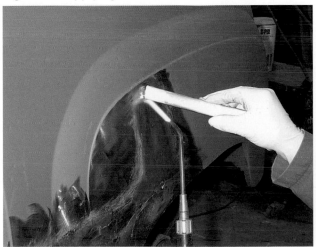

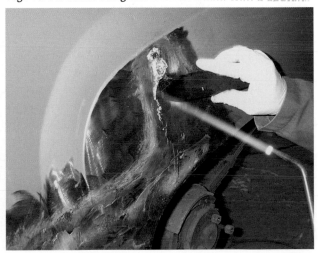

have to be dealt with by very gentle hammering against a dolly held behind, and then filled. Further coats are applied until flatting-off reveals a perfect finish. If working on a large area you will find it helpful to spray a light colour-coat of some sort; this will help the flatting-off process as any low spots will be obvious, since the colour will not be removed by a light rubbing down.

If the bodywork is aluminium you will need to start with a coat of etch primer before using the primer filler; this bites into the metal and keys the rest of the paint to it. This should be followed by a coat of zinc-chromate primer. If it is a coachbuilt body the panels will be hand-formed rather than pressed and therefore not have such a smooth surface, with the consequence that more coats and filling are likely to be required to achieve the surface necessary for the final colour coats of paint. A high-build filler should be used. Etch primer is available in aerosol cans which, as it is quite expensive, will save money if only doing a partial respray.

Glass-fibre bodies may be self-coloured but in most cases will have been painted. If you have had to repair the body and have used a wax-based release agent, all traces of this must be removed by wiping very thoroughly with a cloth soaked in white spirit. But if you used a silicone-based agent then all traces of this must be most carefully removed by flatting off with fine abrasive paper followed by a good wash. Most ordinary primers work well on GRP, but it is worth checking with the supplier before buying. If the pattern from which the GRP was taken had a good finish then the panel or section will have one too and require no more work than a steel panel; otherwise it will need several coats of primer-surfacer and more rubbing down.

Applying these base coats is a good opportunity to develop some skill with the gun and the mixing of paint. The gun should be held at right angles to the surface being treated and moved across it about six to nine inches (15 to 25cm) away from it and parallel to it. If you are too slow you will get a build-up of paint which will sag, and if too quick the coverage will be inadequate. Paint that is too thin will result in runs and paint that is too thick will give you an orange-peel effect. Work on the basis of a double pass of the gun at each application, followed by an interval to allow the solvents to flash off before a further application. Do not be tempted to try for complete coverage by applying too much paint in any one area, this will be achieved with further coats and flatting-off.

It is usual to spray the edges of doors, bonnets, door shuts, etc. before working on the panels. After this, on a saloon, start with the roof, spraying from one side and completing from the other side before continuing with rest of the car.

Minor imperfections in the surface can be filled with cellulose putty – buy it in a tube if you can as it keeps better – used in very thin coats, building up if necessary and leaving it proud of the surface for rubbing down with the rest of the coat when next flatted-off.

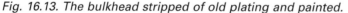

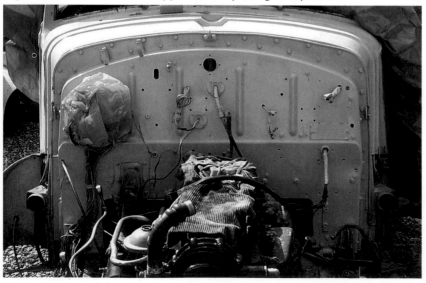

Fig. 16.12. The underbonnet area also needs refinishing.

Fig. 16.13. The bulkhead stripped of old plating and painted.

When you have achieved complete coverage and have a perfect slightly egg-shell finish when rubbed down with, say, 400 grade paper, you can proceed to the colour coats. It is best to do this when the weather is fine and dry, otherwise blooming – the appearance of white patches – can take place.

You will have checked with your supplier whether the finishing coat requires an undercoat or not, but in either case the first coverage of colour needs to be a well-thinned light mist coat to seal the filler, after which two full coats can be sprayed allowing about half an hour to elapse between them. When dry, carefully inspect it and stop up any minor imperfections with the putty, which is followed when dry and flatted-off with two more full colour coats. After allowing this to dry thoroughly, and being satisfied that you have a good solid finish, wipe it with a tack cloth and give it a final thin coat with the paint thinned to about 25% paint and 75% thinners.

This needs time to dry; leave it for several days if you can, but at least for 24 hours. If the coverage is good but the finish disappointing, carefully flat it off with 600 grade paper and then with a really fine grade, such as 1,000 or 1,200, respraying any areas if you cut through the paint, and being very careful on edges, guttering and the like not to rub through to bare metal. Any sags or runs can be dealt with by flatting off and locally respraying if necessary.

Before putting the spray gun away after you have finished using it, empty any surplus paint back into a container, or the paint tin itself (but remember that it has been thinned). Wash out the spray gun container with thinners and spray neat thinners for a few seconds (well away from the job) to clear the nozzle, and wipe the gun clean with a rag soaked in thinners. Make sure that the air hole in the top of the container lid is not clogged-up with dried paint and do not be tempted to immerse the whole gun in thinners as this will harm the seals.

Burnishing or compounding now follows, using the appropriate compound on a slightly damp cloth. This is hard work if you are doing a complete car. An electric polisher with a sponge pad can be used, but take care as it is easy to cut through the colour coats if you are heavy handed. Do not try it with an ordinary electric drill unless you can maintain a slow speed. Excessive speed will generate heat and burn the paint. After finishing with a good polish you should be well rewarded for all your care and hard work.

If you are doing a complete car it's a good idea to detach the doors

Fig. 16.14. Black engine paint used on an inlet manifold.

Fig. 16.15. Wheel discs being prepared for painting – the one on the right has been stripped.

Fig. 16.16. The next stage – the nave plate masked off and the one on the right primed.

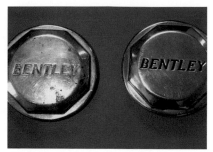

Fig. 16.17. The wheel disc retaining nuts, made of stainless steel, refinished.

and boot and bonnet lids so that you can deal with the edges satisfactorily before spraying the other surfaces, and there may be other areas needing refinishing.

Fig. 16.12 shows an under-the-bonnet view of a badly neglected MkVI Bentley. The bulkhead was originally chromium plated, but this has peeled badly and was partially disguised by a coat of silver Hammerite which was also

peeling. Some of the accessories mounted on the bulkhead have already been removed preparatory to refinishing and the rest will be taken off and each cleaned-up or painted as necessary. Later models of the MkVI had painted bulkheads, so this will be sprayed after proper preparation. It is often necessary to remove the engine to gain access to this area, but in this case it will only be the head that needs

removing (it has to come off anyway) and the manifolds.

Use black engine paint on the head, rocker cover and inlet manifold (see Fig. 16.14) and VHT paint on the exhaust manifold. The cylinder block can also be painted, but must, of course, be thoroughly clean before application.

The wheel discs shown in Fig. 16.15 have a central stainless steel nave plate, but the outer part is painted. These were stripped, the surface prepared with wet-and-dry and primed ready for the colour coats (Fig. 16.16). The Bentley wheel centres, also of stainless steel, were polished and the lettering filled in with a brush (Fig. 16.17).

Fig. 16.18. A Land Rover wing and door being flatted off.

Fig. 16.19. A typical spray gun. The knob at top right controls the shape of the spray fan; the one below it the amount of mix being sprayed, and the one at the bottom of the handle the air pressure.

Fig. 16.20. A door ready for respraying. The rest of the car has been masked with Polymask sheeting. This is anti-static so that it attracts dust away from the areas to be sprayed, and although it allows the part underneath to breathe it is impervious to paint.

Fig. 16.21. Finished. This Dodge pick-up, awaiting its rear body, has just been sprayed in a Bentley polychromatic blue.

Fig. 16.22. A Triumph Herald Coupé refinished in original colours.

Chapter 17

Interior

The feature that everyone looks at more than any other inside a car is the dashboard. On a utility car this may be merely a metal pressing integral to the car's structure, and quite likely sprayed the same colour as the car. Probably all you can do in such a case is to remove or mask off the instruments and switches before refinishing.

On other cars it may be possible to take out the complete dashboard, but before doing so make a sketch of it with the position of the instruments, switches and indicator lights clearly labelled, and disconnect the battery. The dashboard may be screwed directly onto the car's bodywork or be fitted on supporting brackets. Ease it away gently until you can see the back, and support it so that you can work behind it. If you have an oil pressure gauge there will be a copper pipe connecting it to the oil pump or an oil gallery in the engine, and the union connecting it to the gauge will need unscrewing. You may have an oil and/or water temperature gauge connected by a wire-wound capillary tube. These cannot be disconnected from the gauge, and the bulb at the engine end of the tube needs to be removed by undoing its union so that the complete unit can be withdrawn with the instrument or dashboard. These tubes are sealed and, if broken, cannot be repaired, so a complete replacement unit will have to fitted. The capillary tubes are quite fragile and need careful handling. They pass through large grommets in the bulkhead and are usually supported by being clipped to the engine block at intervals.

Earlier cars are likely to have a selection of push/pull switches rather than the later toggle or rocker switches, and they can be unscrewed from the front and pushed though the dash after the knob has been removed, with the wiring intact. On push/pull switches the knobs are often screwed onto the switch, while on rotary switches the knobs will probably fit onto a hexagonal spindle and be retained by a grub screw or a spring-loaded pip which will need depressing with a pointed instrument to allow withdrawal.

Label all the wires and remove the connectors from their terminals. The speedometer drive, if mechanical, will need unscrewing.

The dashboard should now be free and ready for removal, and the stirrups holding the instruments can then be unscrewed to release the instruments along with any remaining fittings. If the dashboard is made of wood it may be a solid piece of hardwood or, more likely, plywood that has been veneered.

Veneering and finishing is dealt with later, but if it is a piece of hardwood and this has split, or you wish to blank off surplus holes, now is the time to make the repairs. Splits can usually be repaired by filling with glue and clamping the board tight so that it closes the split, but if the gap is wide a piece of the wood, including the split, should be sawn out and a well-fitting piece of the same type of wood glued in, matching the grain as closely as possible, and finished to conform to the contours of the board. Similarly, holes can either be plugged with dowel (though they will show the end grain) and stained to the correct colour, or preferably be finished by using a plug to match the grain.

If the dash is metal, or a metal insert which has been detached, it may be plated (which can be renewed), or painted, or it may have a crackle finish. The old paint can be stripped off using Nitromors or similar, ready for respraying. Crackle enamel is available in spray cans from car accessory shops and can give excellent results if the directions are followed carefully.

Some dashboards are made of aluminium, often engine turned to reduce reflection and may be either a solid plate or a thin piece glued to a plywood backing. It will have been varnished or given a coat of clear lacquer to preserve the finish and this can be removed with paint stripper and relacquered after neutralizing it. Incidentally, engine turning is easily done by making a holder to contain a piece of felt or similar of about 1/2in or 3/4in (12mm or 18mm) diameter which is impregnated with fine carborundum paste. This should be rotated quite slowly in a drill press and gently pressed onto the surface of the aluminium, which is marked out in pencil so that each circle is overlapped by half of its diameter. When finished the paste is washed off with petrol or paraffin and the job given a coat of clear lacquer.

Vinyl or leather coating was at

one time a popular finish. This is merely stuck on to a piece of ply, but for a more luxurious feel a thin layer of foam can be sandwiched between them which will give a slightly padded effect to the dashboard when the switches and instruments are refitted.

Some cars with metal dashboards had them painted to represent wood, a technique known as scumbling, in which a lighter colour, to represent the grain and figuring of wood, is painted over a darker colour or vice versa. It is probably easier to veneer such a dash if it has no complicated curves, but if you are a stickler for originality you will have to put in some time practising your scumbling before trying it out on the car.

More modern cars are likely to have a plastic dashboard, probably black, and if this has been neglected, especially if the sun has got at it, it may well be discoloured and faded. There are various preparations available to restore plastic to its original colour which are easily applied; the best one that I have found being colourless but very effective, even on black.

There is a two-part preparation, rather like glass fibre resin, available for restoring damaged

bumpers, that can be used for repairing dashboards and may be useful for filling in unwanted holes. Incidentally, plastic dashboards seem to have a tendency to flex slightly and to rattle, so it is worth looking to see whether yours is secure and, if necessary, provide some insulation, such as foam rubber, at relevant places to prevent chafing or unwanted contact.

INSTRUMENTS AND SWITCHES

Nothing enhances the interior as much as a handsome set of gleaming instruments. Separate instruments usually have their bezels (rims) finished either in chrome plate or matt black paint. In many instances the bezels can be removed by partially rotating them off their case so that the gaps in the bezels line up with the small tongues on the case. This allows the rim to be refinished and the glass to be cleaned – use methylated spirit – on the inside as well as the outside and the dial to be carefully dusted or cleaned. If the dial is in poor condition and you cannot find a replacement, you could make a new one by carefully drawing it in black ink on white

card and using Letraset or similar transfer letters and numbers. Then take a photograph of it and you can have it reduced or enlarged to the exact size – even reversed-out, if needed. If you have a drawing programme on your computer, this would be an even easier and more versatile way of recreating a dial.

Needles, if black, can be repainted in matt paint and, if luminescent, white, unless you have a friendly neighbourhood clockmaker who will touch them in with luminous paint and also repair your clock if it is of the old-fashioned mechanical variety. Take great care, though, as the needles in auxiliary instruments tend to be fragile. Other types of clock will either have a quartz movement or an electro/mechanical movement that uses electric current to tension the spring which actually drives the clockwork movement (known as a remontoire movement) – listen carefully and you will hear it making a sort of slurping noise every few seconds. These aren't something you could repair yourself, and if faulty would need to be replaced, unless you can fit a modern quartz movement behind the existing dial. Other instruments, particularly rev counters and speedometers, need to be repaired and recalibrated professionally.

Switches are often discoloured and, if engraved with identifying letters these are sometimes without their infill paint. Figs. 17.1 and 17.2 show the switch box from a Bentley that has been refurbished together with some switch knobs. The switch box had its paint removed and it was discovered that the engraving for the letters was very shallow. To fill them satisfactorily they were professionally engraved more deeply, then the whole surface sprayed with a cellulose-based engine enamel before being filled with ordinary white paint. It was important to use a different type of paint for filling the engraved letters so as not to dissolve the black

Fig. 17.1. Knobs polished and filled.

Fig. 17.2. Switch box and steering centre ring before refinishing.

paint. The infilling was done with a brush, making sure that there was plenty of paint in the engraving (from which the black paint had been carefully scraped). While still wet, the surplus white paint was wiped off with a pad moistened in white spirit – if it had been cellulose-based the thinners would have wiped off the black paint as well.

The knobs were polished on the buffing wheel, though a good rub with metal polish would have done just as well, and their engraving filled in the same way. The switches themselves were treated to a squirt of WD40, the surplus being wiped off, before being tested and replaced. The main switch box of the Bentley that controls the ignition and lights as well as the starter was found to be faulty when tested, and needed sorting out after 50 years service. I was pleased that I had found this out at this stage rather than after the dash had been replaced and the car rewired, as this would have made fault finding much more difficult.

There is usually a maze of wires behind the dashboard which makes removal and replacement something of a laborious and fiddly job (Fig. 17.3). It is best to make it as self-contained as possible, running the wires connecting the various instruments, lighting and switches in a conduit of plastic tubing, or at least bound together with harness tape (Fig. 17.4), and lead all the cables that are going elsewhere to a multi-plug or plugs, which means that there will be no wrong connections when you put it all together.

Glove boxes should be refurbished. They are usually lined, often with a soft fabric, but are more serviceable with vinyl lining that is easily wiped and less likely to collect dust and fluff.

Later cars will have their instruments grouped together in a binnacle that may comprise separately-cased units, but more probably the various movements are in a single unit connected electrically by means of a printed circuit board instead of wires. There is little you can do to repair these units, so a visit to a breaker's yard may be necessary, but a selection of new faces, in different colours, can be obtained for some models from accessory shops.

Fig. 17.3. An untidy collection of wires behind the dash.

Fig. 17.4. A neater approach to wiring – wires taped and secured.

Fig. 17.5. Veneer damaged by damp.

Fig. 17.6. De-laminated plywood base.

WOOD TRIM

Coachbuilt bodies and mass-produced quality cars had, as many still have, dashboards, door cappings and window framings made of wood. Often these are veneered, using a stable base such as plywood or, on the best quality cars, mahogany; their high polish, along with the leather upholstery and thick carpets, gives a sumptuous feel to the interior. After many years of service, and especially if damp has got into the trim, the polish on the wood dulls, the veneer lifts from the base (Fig. 17.5) and sometimes the plywood base delaminates (Fig. 17.6). All but the most difficult shapes are within the scope of the amateur to refurbish and it is quite entertaining to try one's hand at a different skill.

The various trim items are usually held in place by wood screws which should be removed and the trim lifted away and labelled on the inside if there is likely to be any doubt about replacing it correctly. Examine each piece carefully; any suspicion of rot in the base wood means that it should be replaced or the rot cut out and a new piece glued in. There are many very efficient wood glues available, most of which are stronger than the surrounding wood that they bond, and a waterproof variety should be chosen.

As with other aspects of the car you then have to decide whether to replace or restore. It is sometimes much easier to replace a part with a new one than to restore the old one, and if it is a mechanical part this makes good sense. However, if you value originality, or the car has some special associations, you may wish to restore rather than replace the trim, even though the standard attained may not be as good as a replacement.

The MkV1 Bentley that I am restoring was built for a very well-known person and I decided, therefore, to keep whatever I could that was original, repairing rather than replacing except where there was no alternative.

I carefully removed the damaged veneers with the help of a heat gun on a low setting to melt the glue, after which it was possible to slide a knife blade between the veneer and the base and part the two (Fig. 17.7). As in all the best veneering, the door cappings and dashboard had two veneers on each surface that met in the middle in a butt joint, the two forming what is known in the trade as a 'book match', where each is a mirror image of the other. They

Fig. 17.7. Stripping old veneer.

Fig. 17.8. Laminating strips of wood round a former.

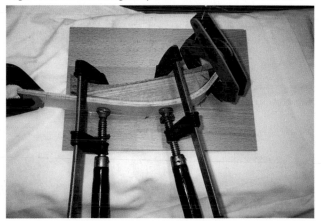

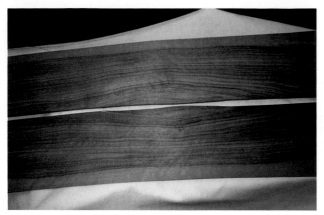

Fig. 17.9. Sheets of veneer – there is a very wide variety available.

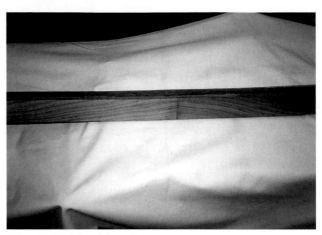

Fig. 17.10. Matching the veneers.

are, as is often the case, of walnut and very well figured, though as the car is a Sportsman's Saloon, the veneering is not as extravagantly executed as in more formal saloons and limousines.

Where necessary I repaired the base wood by letting in new sections of mahogany, or plywood where curved sections were required. I glued several layers of plywood together and clamped them to formers which had been cut to the correct curvature (Fig. 17.8).

A very wide variety of wood is used for veneering and you need to choose the right type for the job. It is not sufficient merely to specify 'walnut' as several quite different types are in use. However, if you take a sample to your suppliers they should be able to identify it. Alternatively, send for a pack of samples from which you can select

the correct type. Veneers are supplied in several different sizes of sheet (Fig. 17.9).

If, as in my case, most of the parts only required a half section of veneer, I spent some time trying to get the best possible match of the grain to achieve something like the 'book match' effect (Fig. 17.10). It would have been easier, and made for a more perfect result, if I had replaced all the veneers. However, as the original was not too exotic, I made reasonable matches, and I cut the new pieces slightly oversize whenever possible.

Depending on the type of wood, especially very highly figured walnut, veneers can be brittle and prone to come apart along the grain. This does not matter too much on long straight pieces, since when glued and bound together the veneers will close, but if there

are curves or more intricate work is involved it is best either to soak the veneer in water until it becomes pliable, or steam it. Bind it to the base while it is still wet and do not glue it until it has thoroughly dried, when it should fit perfectly The professionals use heat and a vacuum to achieve this.

The type of glue you use is important. Impact adhesives are no good because you need time to manipulate and smooth the veneer, and you also may need to stain the veneer or touch it in with wood dye to enhance the match. If the glue will not take stain, then any that forces its way to the surface or at the joins will be obvious. Craft shops that sell veneers also sell glues that are suitable.

The veneer is glued and clamped or bound with masking tape to the base wood (Fig. 17.11).

Fig. 17.11. Binding the veneer to its base.

Fig. 17.12. Clamps can be used on straight sections.

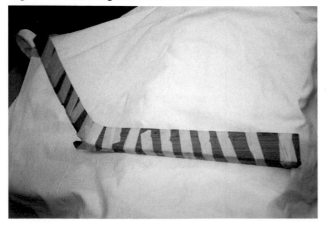

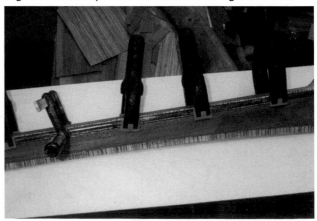

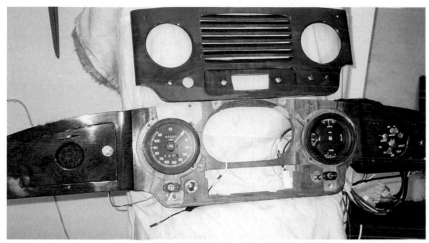

Fig. 17.13. The dashboard, in two parts.

quartered on large areas, and some had more than one type of veneer, sometimes in patterns which are often works of art on their own. The Bentley, as will be seen from the illustrations, has the walnut door cappings edged with a different wood (called Zebrano because of its stripes). Much of this had to be renewed, which was slightly awkward as it meant cutting across the grain to make the strips, but at least they did not have to be matched!

The dashboard is in two parts, the centre section (Fig. 17.13) fitting over the instruments. The apertures are bevelled (Fig. 17.14) and although they can be veneered they are often painted in dark brown instead; these had been originally, so were sanded down and given several coats.

When thoroughly dry it can be trimmed using a craft knife or a model maker's plane for smoothing along the edge of the grain; very minor imperfections can be filled with wood filler which is available in colours to suit different types of wood.

In many cases the highest quality cars had veneering that was

Fig. 17.14. Bevelled instrument apertures, painted.

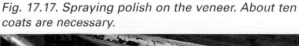

Fig. 17.15. New door capping, sanded ready for polishing. Note Zebrano banding.

Fig. 17.16. Removing the old polish.

Fig. 17.17. Spraying polish on the veneer. About ten coats are necessary.

When all the cutting and glueing is finished the work can be smoothed down (Fig. 17.15) using fine sand paper, preferably on a block, especially if there are different types of wood since the softer will rub away more than the harder and leave hollows which will be noticeable when polished.

Older polishes tend not to wear well, especially if not cared for, and modern polishes are very much easier to apply and much harder-wearing. Polish can be removed, like paint, by using a paint remover, but be careful to neutralize it after use (Fig. 17.16). Suppliers will recommend a finish that is suitable, but Rustin's Plastic Coating (a two-pack preparation) or Craftlac Melamine (a cellulose-based finish) are good. It is said that they can be applied by brush, but my experience is that a small spray gun is more effective (Fig. 17.17). A number of thin coats are needed to build up to the required finish. The Rustin's takes longer to dry than the Craftlac Melamine which can have a double pass of the spray gun at intervals of about 20 minutes. However, both need to be flatted off at intervals to remove runs, bubbles or other imperfections, using 600 grade wet-and-dry paper or the finest grade of wire wool. Various trials showed that the polish should be thinned by the addition of about 30% of thinners and a low air pressure of about 40psi produced the best results. About ten coats seem to be needed to give a solid, high gloss polish.

Most cars with wood trim, and especially the closed saloons and limousines, had a very high gloss finish indeed (Figs. 17.18 and 17.19) but not all, some preferring an egg-shell finish. The amount of the preparation you apply will be the same in either case; it is the last part of the process that determines the level of gloss. For the deepest, shiniest finish the final coat, when really thoroughly dry, is flatted-off very gently with very fine steel

Figs. 17.18 and 17.19. A high gloss finish.

Fig. 17.20. A collection of dashboard templates.

Fig. 17.21. A new dashboard in ply, sanded ready for veneering.

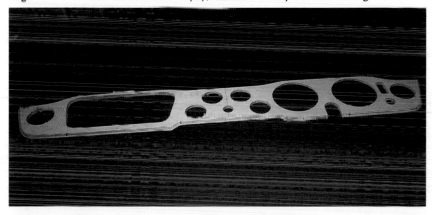

wool or 1,200 grade wet-and-dry and then burnished with normal cutting-in paste or T-Cut. This gives a deep gloss shine which is then further enhanced by a coat of wax or car polish. The egg-shell finish is

Fig. 17.22. Burr walnut veneers selected as suitable for the instrument panel.

obtained by a very light smoothing with fine – 1,200 or 1,500 wet-and-dry paper followed by polishing.

Wood trim is usually held in place by means of chromium-plated raised-head screws – countersunk but with a slightly domed head, with screw cups under the heads. (Be choosy about the quality of the screw cups, many of them are of poor quality with a minimal deposit of chrome plating.) These screws have become very difficult to source and you may find it easier to obtain the stainless steel self-tappers. These have the advantage that, being parallel for most of their length, they won't split the wood and, of course, they can secure the trim to metal. The trim on some later cars is held in place by means of clips.

The sequence of photographs (Figs. 17.20 to 17.29) shows how the professionals go about restoring interior woodwork. Where the damage or delamination of the base wood is too extensive to repair, a new part is made in the same type of wood as the original. If the original base wood is too far gone to copy (or is missing) a suitable template is chosen from stock. Veneers are carefully selected for the particular part, especially if the 'book match' effect is required, and cut out with a knife after being marked out in pencil. The base and veneer are then glued and bound together with masking tape. Since most wood trim is not flat but contoured – even instrument apertures are often veneered on their bevels – some method of creating even pressure over the whole area is necessary, so a vacuum bed is used and the parts placed on it. They are then covered with a rubber sheet, the edges of which are clamped down to make a seal, which, when the air is evacuated, moulds itself to the contours of the trim being veneered and maintains a steady pressure until the bond is complete. The bed is warmed to help the

Fig. 17.23. Cutting out the veneers.

Fig. 17.24. Veneer, glued to base wood, taped to a support plank and placed on a vacuum bed.

forming of the veneer and the setting of the adhesive.

After this operation the work is sanded smooth ready for the application of the polish, which is normally done by spraying. This is carried out in a booth which is heated to maintain the right temperature, and the air is constantly evacuated to remove the overspray. Fig. 17.27 shows this process.

Fig. 17.25. Veneered wood in place on vacuum bed covered with a sheet of rubber.

Fig. 17.26. Vacuum applied which, together with warm air, ensures veneer conforms to shape of base wood and is securely glued.

Fig. 17.27. Spraying the polish. Note the safety precautions – overalls, gloves and air-fed mask.

Fig. 17.28. Burnishing – a light touch is needed.

Fig. 17.29. From right to left – before; with new veneer applied; after polishing and burnishing.

The sprayed parts are left overnight to allow time for hardening, then thoroughly inspected. At this stage the polish is cloudy and needs buffing to bring out its gloss. This is done with a fabric wheel impregnated with a fine polishing compound, and care has to be taken as it is easy to overdo things and cut through the polish to the veneer itself. A well done job will produce a finish like glass.

TRIM PANELS

Trim panels on the doors and the inside of the body are usually made of millboard with vinyl covering or, on the best quality cars, Bedford cord or leather covering, often patterned. Dampness takes its toll of millboard over time, especially in open cars, and buckling is a common problem (Fig. 17.30). Panels will be either screwed or clipped to the door frames or bodywork. When removing them you must first take off any door or window furniture, together with armrests if there are any. Armrests are often held in position by carefully hidden screws that go through to the inside door skin, while window winder handles may be held by a circlip or a pin

(Fig. 17.31). In the latter case the pin is retained by the decorative bezel which is spring-loaded; push the bezel towards the panel against its spring and with a pointed instrument push out the pin from the base of the handle.To pop off clipped-on panels, carefully prize up the clips (probably made of plastic and easily broken) using two screwdrivers (one either side of each clip) or the special forked tool for this purpose (Fig. 17.32).

Having carefully removed whatever covering it has you can use the panel as a template. If it is a door panel it will have holes in it to accommodate the window winder and the door handle, and if it is held in place by clips there will be a series of holes around the edge where the clips fit. Whatever type the clips are (and especially if they are poppers) it is important that the holes are placed accurately otherwise the clips will not register with their mating holes in the door or bodywork.

If the covering is patterned vinyl it can be hard to reproduce since it is done by a heat and pressure process in manufacture, so in such cases if you really want to keep to the original look you will probably have to seek replacements. However, the patterns in cord or leather can be sewn if you have a machine that will cope with it.

Millboard may not be obtainable, but thin (3mm) MDF can be used instead as a backing. If the panel is curved, choose

Fig. 17.30. A buckled millboard door trim.

Fig. 17.31. The components of a window winder.

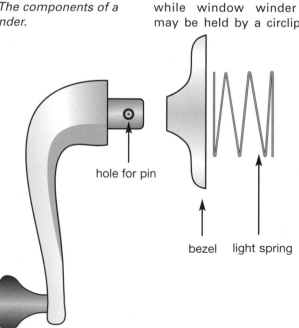

hole for pin

bezel   light spring

Fig. 17.32. A forked lever for lifting door trim and body trim clips.

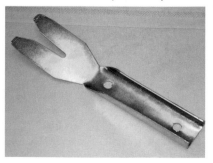

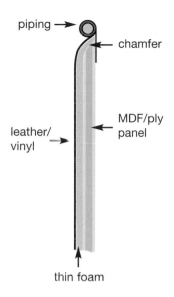

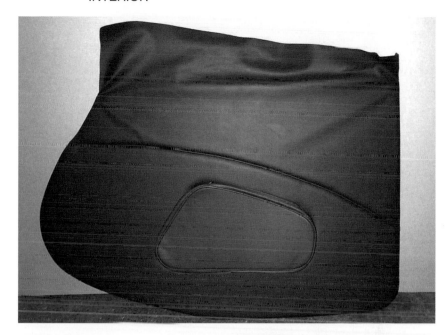

Fig. 17.33. Chamfered trim with piping.

hardboard – although thin plywood is more rigid and less likely to be affected by water. If you do use plywood, pick marine ply or outdoor quality as it is waterproof. By chamfering the edge and running piping around it you can make a very neat and professional looking job of it (Fig. 17.33). A thin lining of foam sandwiched between the covering and the board also gives it an air of quality and adds some noise insulation to the panel.

Map pockets can be added either on the surface (if there is room) or let into the panels by cutting out an appropriate aperture in the panel and attaching a shallow box to the inside. Having made the box, cover it with whatever trim material you are using before fitting it, and make sure that any in-door mechanisms (especially wind-down windows) don't snag on it.

The covering can be stapled to the rear of the panel. Figs. 17.34 and 17.35 show an almost completed panel with pocket; the covering is left long at the top because it fits under a wooden door capping, and a little extra here gives a good grip for tensioning the cover before it is pulled over and stapled.

Figs. 17.34 and 17.35. Door panel with pocket.

SEATS

The reconstruction of car upholstery is a skilled job, but it is perfectly possible for the amateur to make new covers for existing seating, and a domestic sewing machine will cope with most materials. The seat covers just visible in the photograph of the Singer Sports Nine in the Introduction were made of vinyl material that closely resembled leather and were the author's first attempt at upholstery. They came out well, even though only the seat frames existed and there were no patterns to follow.

The illustrations show the professionals doing the job. The material, leather in this case, with a lining of foam, is first marked out, using the original as patterns for the various panels, then cut out.

Fig. 17.36. A hide – a complete skin.

Leather is bought by the hide, literally a complete skin (Fig. 17.36) treated and dyed. Figs. 17.37 – 17.42 show the various parts required for a seat base for a Mk V Jaguar. Patterns for the various new panels are taken from the old ones. Generally, to make the patterns, it is best to unpick the panels from the passenger side seat, as this is usually less worn.

The finished panels are then sewn together. It is very common to use piping at the edges of the panels, often in a contrasting colour. This is simply made by wrapping a strip of the covering over a cord or nylon core, and sewing it together with a special foot on a sewing machine, or it can be glued.

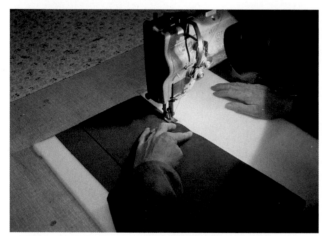

Fig. 17.37. The flutes are first sewn into a panel...

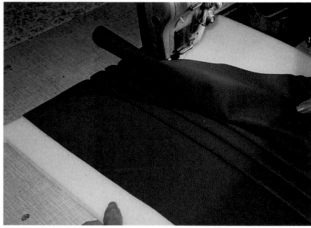

Fig. 17.38. ... together with the backing foam.

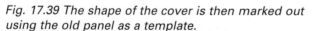

Fig. 17.39 The shape of the cover is then marked out using the old panel as a template.

Fig. 17.40 The calico 'frog' is stapled to the wooden strips secured to the metal squab.

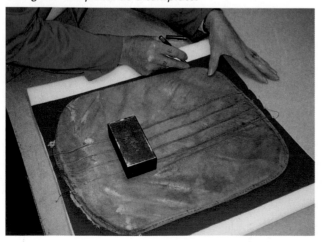

Fig. 17.41 The leather cover is stretched over the frame, ...

Fig. 17.42 ... and then attached with 'hog rings' using special pliers.

The backing foam is itself backed by calico. When assembling the seat, the calico is first secured to the wooden strips, which are attached to the metal frame with staples, before the cover itself is eased over the frame. When the cover is smoothed and positioned satisfactorily, it is secured to the metal frame using metal 'hog' rings which require special pliers to close them. Undamaged leather upholstery can often be improved by the use of saddle soap or a proprietary cleaner, but if damaged or badly cracked it will need replacing. However, it is by no means always necessary to replace the complete cover, as new panels can be let in to replace damaged ones and then refinished to match the original. The Aston seats (Fig. 17.43) have had some new panels let into the squabs that are completely undetectable from the original because they have been recoloured.

Fig. 17.43. Refurbished Aston Martin seats that have had new panels let into the squabs.

Above left: Fig. 17.44. Sewing edging onto the carpets.

Above right: Fig. 17.45. Mitring the corners.

Right: Fig. 17.46. Construction of a traditional seat with wood and horsehair.

Below: Fig. 17.47. A felt and lead sandwich underlay from an Aston Martin.

Fig. 17.48. Interiors as they used to be. A 1913 Unic with railway type embroidered window lifts.

Fig. 17.49. Buttoned upholstery. Rear seat of the 1913 Unic being replaced. Not much call for it today, but a splendid example of the upholsterer's skill.

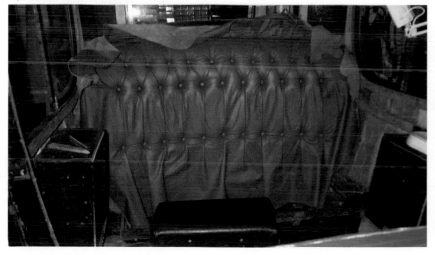

CARPETS

Carpeting comes in different grades, from the very cheap ready-made replacements of rubber-backed nylon for small sports cars to the expensive Wilton such as that used in an Aston Martin and other expensive cars. The old carpets are used as patterns wherever possible, to save time, and the new material cut out accordingly, then bound to stop the edges fraying and to give a good appearance. Strips are cut from the hide that is being used for the seats and sewn along the edges (Fig. 17.44) the corners being mitred (Fig. 17.45). After sewing, a very sharp knife and a very steady hand are used to cut off the surplus leather close to the seam. An underlay is used, often rubber-backed, between the floor of the car and the carpet both for feel and for sound insulation. The Aston Martin had a felt underlay with a sheet of lead sandwiched between two layers (Fig. 17.47) to give maximum sound deadening.

Fig. 17.50. A later coat, from a mass-produced car, with a metal frame.

HEADLININGS

On modern cars headlinings tend to be a sheet of plastic with insulation material as backing, pressed and formed to shape and then glued in place, but earlier cars had headlinings that were cut to size and then tacked to wooden frame members or sewn on to a metal frame. If you have such a lining and it will not clean up with chemical cleaners or steam cleaning, and you are determined to do it yourself, the best advice is to remove it very carefully and note how it was held in place originally. This is the sort of job that I would put out to be done professionally but it is likely to be expensive.

HOODS

On cheaper sports cars hoods are generally made of vinyl, while for the more expensive cars a material known as double duck is used, and on the even more expensive cars you may find them made of mohair. If the original is to hand for use as a pattern, diy hood-making is within the scope of an amateur, but it is much more difficult to get it right without a template. Padded hoods that have headlining incorporated are a very different proposition, and great care and skill, which only comes with experience, is required to achieve a precise fit which is evenly padded and wrinkle free.

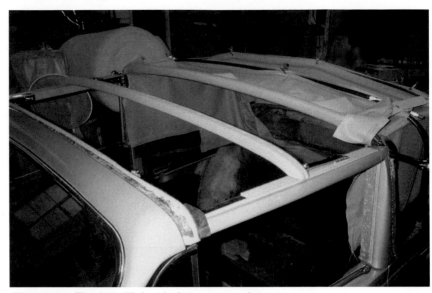

Fig. 17.51. The headlining being prepared.

Fig. 17.52. The headlining fitted temporarily to the rails.

Fig. 17.53. The headlining being tacked into place.

Fig. 17.54. The rear half of the headlining is padded.

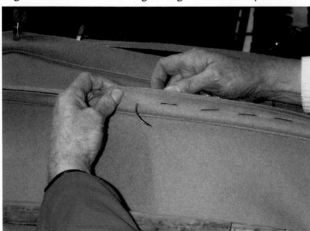

142

Fig. 17.55. The outer cover panels being measured.

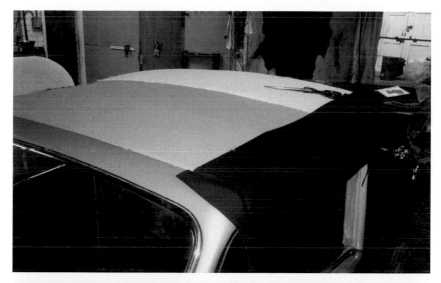

Figs. 17.51 to 17.57 show the professionals at work. First the headlining is cut out, leaving plenty to spare, and pegged to the rails after the webbing straps that hold the rails in place have been fitted. The lining is then tacked to the rails using a curved upholsterer's needle. This Mk5 Jaguar is a drophead coupé, and as the front half of the hood folds to the half-way position, only the rear part of the roof is padded, otherwise it would be too bulky when the whole of the roof is folded.

The outer covering, double duck in this case, is cut into panels before being sewn and finally fitted.

Fig. 17.56. The finished hood.

Fig. 17.57. The interior. The straps are for holding the rolled back front roof when in the 'de Ville' position.

Chapter 18

Plating

One of the few jobs to do with car restoration that an amateur cannot undertake is plating, and this is because of the plant and equipment that's needed to apply nickel or chrome plate to components. However, a brief description of the process may be of interest and may explain why it is relatively expensive.

Before sending components for re-plating, make any necessary repairs, knocking out dents or other imperfections, or alternatively, filling them with weld or brazing. Check that any joints are sound, as if you have to heat them after plating, you will destroy the new plating. Assemblies of several parts will have to be dismantled into their separate parts.

Clean up any repairs, and the worst of any rust or pitting, using a file or an abrasive disc. This will save the metal polisher time, and you money, but do ensure that the basic shape of the component is retained, and do not round-off edges or create localised depressions.

The first thing metal polishers will do is strip the existing plating, paint and any other impurities from the components you have sent them. They do this by immersing the parts for about 20 minutes in a sulphuric acid bath (Fig. 18.1), after which they will wash them in water. When dry, they will grind or linish them with a fine abrasive to remove any surface imperfections and then polish them on a hard (sewn) mop or wheel (Fig. 18.2) with a medium abrasive to remove the linishing marks, before polishing to a bright

Fig. 18.1. A sulphuric acid bath for removing old plating, paint, etc.

Fig. 18.2. Polishing using a hard (sewn) mop or wheel.

finish with a soft (loose) mop and fine abrasive. Fig. 18.3 shows wheel locking nuts, one of which has been linished and the other polished.

This is the end of the polishing process and the parts will now be immersed for about five minutes in the first of a number of baths – this first one is to remove any grease deposited by the abrasive. Next they are washed in water (this happens between each stage of the process) and then electrically cleaned in another bath (anodic for steel and cathodic for non-ferrous metals). A dip in a 10% sulphuric bath follows before the first of the three deposits – copper (on steel), nickel and chrome – takes place.

The copper deposit is an acid solution for steel (or cyanide for diecast metal) and takes only a few minutes; after washing the parts are immersed in the nickel tank for about 40 minutes and they emerge bright plated; another wash and they are put in the chrome tank for just three to four minutes. From this they emerge with a bright golden finish (Fig. 18.4) but this is only the colour of the solution which is washed off leaving the bright chromium finish that is the end product of this very specialised process (Fig. 18.5).

Top: Fig. 18.3. Wheel locking nuts – one polished, one linished.

Middle: Fig. 18.4. A plated frame being lifted from the final bath (it's the plating solution clinging to it that gives the frame its temporary golden hue).

Bottom: Fig. 18.5. A plated frame after its final wash in water.

Chapter 19

Workshop practice

Some of the more common workshop tasks are dealt with here, and it is worth remembering that if you are unable to do anything yourself there will be somebody who can. I have always found that the professionals are sympathetic and helpful to the amateur, both in sharing their knowledge and undertaking specific jobs, often only for a 'drink' if they are not too time consuming and especially if they can be fitted in with other, more profitable jobs.

FASTENERS

There is a very wide range of fasteners, and some of those most commonly used on motor vehicles are shown in Fig. 19.1. Nearly all nuts and bolts have a right-hand thread. Threads that are left-handed are likely to be used only on rotating parts that might tend to unscrew with the direction of rotation, as noted in the chapter on wheels. If you have difficulty in loosening a nut or bolt it is always worth checking that it does not have a left-hand thread.

Ordinary nuts usually have a washer under them; and if it is important that they do not unscrew they will have a locking device such as a spring washer or a self-locking nut. Self-locking nuts must never be reused. If it is vitally important that a nut does not unscrew, it can be locked by means of a split pin through a drilled hole in the bolt and slots in the nut, the arms of the pin being secured as shown in Fig. 19.1.

Shafts may be retained by use of circlips, fitted internally or externally, and pulleys, gears or wheels that transmit motion may be secured to their shafts or hubs by keys, tapers or splines, or sometimes by a mixture of a taper and a key.

Always clean round any two parts that are fitted together if you are uncertain as to how they mate, so that you can decide on the proper method of undoing them.

TAPS AND DIES

Threads are formed by using taps in holes and dies on rods and bolts. They come in the same sizes and threads as nuts and bolts and a small set of the appropriate type for the vehicle on which you are working is often very helpful as not only can you make fasteners but, and perhaps more important, you can clean up corroded ones very simply.

Taps come in three types per size – taper, second and parallel. An engineering works might use all three but only the taper and the parallel are necessary for our purpose; the taper to start the thread in a hole and the parallel tap to finish it. The hole to be threaded needs to be undersize and you will have to obtain a chart that gives the various tapping and clearing sizes (Fig. 19.2).

When using a tap (Fig. 19.5) fit it to the handle and make sure that it is upright in the hole. Applying slight pressure, turn it slowly for about half a revolution at a time and then back off by a few degrees to clear the swarf that it has made. When through the hole, or as far as you can go into a blind hole, the taper tap is unwound and followed by the parallel tap. A few drops of oil help when tapping steel, or paraffin on brass.

To cut threads on an external surface the die is fitted to its holder with the tapered side downwards, the locking screw tightened, and placed on the end of the rod which should have a slight taper filed on it to lead the die (Fig. 19.4). It is essential to keep the die at right angles to the work otherwise a deformed thread will result. As with the tap, about half a revolution is made before backing off a few degrees. If the resultant thread is very tight in its hole, the central locking screw in the die holder should be slackened off and the two small grub screws either side of it tightened to reduce its diameter slightly, and the rod rethreaded at this setting.

Opposite: Fig. 19.1. A range of fasteners commonly used on motor vehicles.

Below: Fig. 19.2. Tapping chart, giving drill sizes for taps.

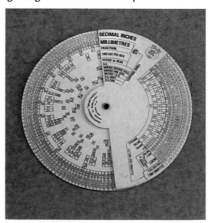

Full nut

Half nut
or lock nut

Castle nut

Slotted nut

Self-locking nut
with nylon insert

Split pin fitted with castle nut

Plain
washer

Spring
washer

Split pin

Roll pin

Bolt

Setscrew

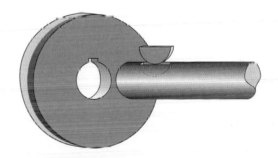
Key in shaft, keyway in pulley

Cap head socket screw

Blind or 'pop' rivet

Circlip

Countersunk socket screw

Circlip (alternative type)

Fig. 19.3. Taps, dies and holders.

Fig. 19.4. A die in use, extending the thread on a bolt.

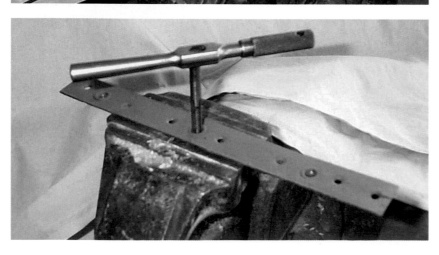

Fig. 19.5. Using a tap to clear a corroded thread.

BUSH REMOVAL AND REFITTING

Bushes are (usually) seamless tubes with a smooth bore for a shaft to revolve or slide in. They are replaceable items, used to avoid having to replace a larger or more valuable component to which they are fitted, and they are normally made of bronze or steel. Bushes are held in place by being made very slightly larger than the hole into which they inserted. The fit is known as an interference fit, and because of this they have to be forced in or out of their housings, and care needs to be taken not to deform them. Where great precision is required bushes need to be reamed to the correct size after being fitted.

A shouldered punch (Fig. 19.6) is a useful tool for removing a bush, the shoulders bearing on the bush itself (being fractionally smaller on its outside diameter) and the central portion acting as a guide, the punch being either driven with a hammer or in a press. A vice makes a good press for small items. If the new bush is not too tight a fit in its housing it may be replaced in the same way. If it is tight, either to replace or to remove, you will probably do better using a length of studding (threaded rod) or a long bolt. This method requires a tube (Fig. 19.7)

slightly larger in diameter than the bush to act as a spacer as it is withdrawn (a socket will do if the bush is short – Fig. 19.8) and a stout washer or plate placed under the head of the bolt. As the nut is tightened the bush is drawn – or withdrawn – into or out of its housing; this is a much more gentle method than the punch and hammer.

In cases where there is difficulty in withdrawing the bush, the surrounding metal may be heated as this may break the 'stiction' of the components, but if this is not possible and there is sufficient room, a hacksaw blade threaded through the bush will cut through it and make it easy to drive it out.

If the bush is loose in its housing, perhaps because of it having seized on its shaft, the remedy is usually to drill or ream out the hole to ensure that it is round and to make an oversize bush. If for some reason this cannot be done it may be possible to build up the component with weld and redrill the hole to the original size of the bush.

GASKETS

There are many instances when a gasket is used between mating parts to seal them against the loss of compression, lubricant, gas or water – sometimes these may also

act as spacers in which case their thickness can be important.

Engine gaskets are usually sold in complete sets, for top or complete overhaul, and include the all important cylinder-head gasket. A very few cars had the head and block lapped together so that they mated absolutely accurately, thus precluding the need for a gasket, but these were normally racing or very high performance engines. If you are unable to obtain a new head gasket you may be able to resurrect the old one, if it is of the copper and asbestos type, by heating both faces to a dull red heat and plunging it in water to anneal, or soften it. If it is missing or too badly damaged to be reused, you can make a new one out of a thin sheet of copper, using as a template the old gasket (if available) or making a paper pattern from the cylinder head. Copper sheet of 18swg (standard wire gauge) thickness should be used and it should be annealed before being fitted.

It will not take up as much unevenness as a copper-asbestos gasket and you should ensure that both the cylinder head and the mating surface of the block are flat by having them milled. If necessary, a smear of gasket cement will enhance its effectiveness.

If other gaskets are not available they are easily made from the

Fig. 19.6. A shouldered punch to remove a bush.

Fig. 19.7. Length of studding with tube as spacer to withdraw a bush.

Fig. 19.8. A socket used as spacer for the withdrawal of a bush.

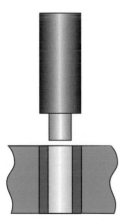

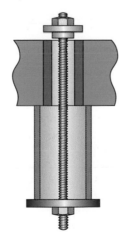

appropriate materials, available either from accessory shops or motor factors. There are different types of gasket material which are sold in sheet form. A rubber/cork material, which is relatively thick and has plenty of give in it, is used where one of the components is of pressed steel, such as a rocker cover or sump where there may be inaccuracies to be taken up. Oil paper, available in different thicknesses, is used between machined surfaces such as thermostat housings and a graphited material, also available in different thicknesses, where there is some pressure from oil or water.

The shape of the component or flange for which the gasket is being made should be traced onto the material, which, if not too thick, can be cut with scissors, but with a complex shape with thin walls and bolt holes close to them this requires considerable delicacy and the use of a ball pein hammer is to be preferred.

The gasket material is held over the component and is tapped, using the ball of the hammer, around the edges of the component (Fig. 19.9). This traps the material between the two metal surfaces and cuts it very neatly. Small holes are cut by supporting the component, placing the ball of the hammer over the hole and tapping it with a second hammer. A set of wad punches (Fig. 19.10) [originally so called as they were used for cutting the wads that held the firing charge in muzzle-loading guns] is very helpful for making the smaller holes, and almost essential for making washers out of red fibre material for seals on pipelines.

Fig. 19.9. Gasket-making using a ball pein hammer.

Fig. 19.10. A selection of wad punches for making holes for studs, bolts, etc.

METAL JOINING

Metal joining by the use of heat falls into three categories, soldering, brazing (both of which use a third metal to make the bond) and welding (which melts the two metals to be joined).

SOLDERING

Soldering is particularly useful for joining together non-ferrous metals like brass and copper and thin sheet tin plate and mild steel. Solder, an alloy of tin and lead, is available in strip or wire form of various thicknesses and grades, some melting at a lower temperature than others. A flux is required to prevent oxidization and to help the solder to flow; in wire-type solder this is often incorporated as a core in the wire itself, but otherwise is available in liquid form such as Baker's Fluid, or paste, such as Fluxite. The liquid form is particularly useful for large areas, the paste for smaller ones and for electrical connections. Both are corrosive if left and any surplus should be washed off after the job has been done.

Many people seem to find soldering difficult, and the secret lies in the preparation of the metal surfaces and getting them, as well as the solder, to the right heat. The two pieces of metal must be absolutely clean where they are to be joined and should be made bright with the use of emery cloth or steel wool and then coated with flux; you can use either a soldering iron or a blowlamp to provide the required heat.

Soldering irons come in different sizes, the smaller ones being electrically heated and the others requiring an external heat source, such as a blowlamp, to heat the bit (the copper end which retains the heat) to the right temperature, which is easily recognised as the flame turns a bright green when it is reached. The bit should first be tinned by cleaning it on emery cloth then dipping it in the flux. On applying solder to it, this melts and coats the tip of the bit which is placed in contact with the metals to heat them to the melting point of the solder, which is then brought into contact with both and runs into the heated joint.

On larger areas, a blowlamp flame may be used to heat the joint, the solder being applied directly to the metal, when it will run into the hottest part. A solder paste is available that consists of flux impregnated with particles of solder which can be painted on to the respective metals which are then clamped or otherwise held together while being heated to the melting point of the solder. This is particularly useful when soldering large areas or those which are difficult to get at with an iron, but only moderate heat should be used; excessive heat will tend to burn the flux and make soldering impossible.

Aluminium can only be soldered with special flux and solder and needs special care not to overheat.

BRAZING

This, like soldering, uses a third metal to create the bond between the items being joined, but operates at a much higher temperature and therefore is used on heavier gauge material and

forms a much stronger bond. The same meticulous preparation of the pieces to be joined is necessary. The medium used is usually an amalgam of copper and tin (bronze) but often with other metals added to improve its strength. Brazing rods, or spelter, are obtainable in different heat ranges for different purposes and there is also a variety of fluxes, though some rods contain their own flux, and for general purposes household borax makes a good flux. Flux generally comes as a powder and is mixed with a small quantity of clean water to make a paste that is painted onto the prepared joint before heating to make it adhere. The rod is heated slightly and dipped into the powdered flux (if the rod is not flux impregnated) before being applied to the joint, which should be heated to a dull red colour, at which point the rod melts and runs into the joint.

When cooled the joint should be scrubbed with a wire brush to remove any residual flux which has a glass-like appearance and hardness.

The equipment required for brazing depends on the thickness and type of material being joined. Thin sections, even of mild steel can be satisfactorily heated with an ordinary gas blowtorch, but for thicker sections a gas-and-oxygen fed torch is required (Fig. 19.11). Kits with small canisters of oxygen and gas are available but if you intend to do a lot of brazing it will be more economical to hire cylinders from industrial gas suppliers.

Silver soldering is a form of brazing, but at a lower temperature range, the spelter being an amalgam of silver which melts at a lower temperature than bronze. It is available in different heat ranges and is used for delicate work, usually on non-ferrous metals.

There is also a proprietary product (Limiweld) available for joining aluminium and alloys and building-up broken sections.

WELDING

The earliest form of welding required the heating of the parts to be joined to white heat and hammering them, using silver sand as flux, to bond them together – but things have moved on since then. Gas welding, using equipment similar to that for brazing but at a higher temperature, is much used, as is electric arc welding. Both still have their place, but for motor vehicle work they have become largely superseded by shielded-gas arc welding (Mig) which is especially useful for welding thin sections, such as body panels, and creates little distortion as the heat generated is very localized.

The equipment consists of an arc welder and a supply of welding gas (CO_2), and works by feeding a wire from a reel through the torch to the work, which is earthed to the welder. The tip of the wire forms an electric arc with the earthed workpiece which melts the metal, the wire also melting to form a filler. This takes place within a shield of gas which prevents oxidization and aids the welding process.

Preparation need not be as thorough as in the other two processes, but rust, grease, paint and other impurities must be removed otherwise the weld will be porous – no flux is necessary.

Gas can be obtained in small canisters but, as with brazing, if you intend to do much of it a larger rented gas bottle is a must. However, some equipment works without a separate supply of gas as this is generated by the special flux-cored wire that is used. This welding wire is considerably more expensive than the ordinary type, and limited to the welding of mild steel, but may be worth considering. You will need to buy a dual purpose Mig welder to make use of it.

The light emitted by the electric-arc welding process is intense and if not properly protected you can

Fig. 19.11. Gas and oxygen welding/brazing equipment.

get 'arc eye', and exposure to the rays can also affect your skin. A shield must always be used when welding. This may be hand-held or fitted to the head with a strap and should have a very dark lens through which the weld can be seen when the arc is struck. Lenses come in different grade of density, those numbered 8 to 11 being in general use, 8 being less dense than 11 and therefore easier to see through, which is useful when starting the weld.

Leather welder's gauntlets should be worn to preserve the hands from the sparks that sometimes occur during the welding process.

Aluminium and stainless steel can also be welded, but different wires are used and argon gas instead of CO_2.

A wide variety of equipment is available. A welding set with a capacity of about 130 amps is suitable for most restoration work and can be operated from an ordinary 13 amp socket. Instructions are included with new sets, but briefly the process is as follows and a few practice runs should be made on scrap of various thicknesses before you

start in earnest. Indeed, experienced welders always try out the settings of the welder each time they use it and make any necessary adjustments.

Plug in the welder and attach its earth clip to the work, turn on the gas at the canister or bottle – it does not feed from the nozzle until the trigger is pressed. If there is a graduated scale on the tap controlling the flow set it to 10 to start with.

On the welder there are switches to select the voltage, which depends on the thickness of the material to be welded – if in doubt start with the lowest, otherwise you may blow the edge of the metal away. A rotary control varies the current setting and the wire speed; if it is too fast it will tend to push the torch away from the work. The tip of the wire should be held at about 5mm from the work and at right angles to it but with the torch angled at about 60° sideways, and then moved steadily along the joint, maintaining the distance of the tip to the workpiece, and the angle. On a long weld the two pieces should be tack welded at the beginning and end to hold them in position, and on very thin material additional small tacks should be made at intervals to spread the heat.

There is, of course, much more to it than that, but this will get you going and practice will make you proficient. Safety precautions are paramount, first to yourself and then to your surroundings, so if you are welding on the car ensure that petrol and oil, and flammable materials like plastic trim cannot be affected, and have a bucket of water standing by. Finally, and especially if you are about to lock up and leave the workshop or garage, do be absolutely sure that a spark has not landed somewhere where there is flammable material and is smouldering away ready to burst into flames after you have left.

Use an angle grinder to fettle or neaten the weld when finished. Be sure to wear protective goggles and gloves.

METAL POLISHING

One way of finishing metal is simply by polishing – it is a treatment much used on aluminium and its alloys but equally applicable to brass, copper and steel. Indeed, pre-war racing cars such as Bugattis had the front suspension components highly polished, instead of plated or painted, so that any hairline cracks could be easily detected, and it is quite wrong when rebuilding to concours d'élégance standards to have them chromium plated, though perhaps understandable as it saves constant attention to the finish to prevent them from rusting.

Brass and copper pipes and fittings look good when polished, as do aluminium rocker covers and SU carburettor suction chambers, but it is easy to overdo things, and once having polished them they need fairly frequent attention to keep them bright, although clear lacquer can be applied provided it is not in contact with heat.

Alloy wheels are common and need periodic attention as they suffer from weather and road grit. They can be sent away to be dealt with but are easily refurbished at home, and the procedure described holds true for other components.

Depending on their condition, particularly near the rim, you may be able to repolish them without removing the tyres. The first thing to do is to wash the wheels well to remove mud and road dirt which contains coarse grit that will scratch the alloy during the polishing process. Polished alloy wheels are often protected by transparent lacquer, which can lift (Fig. 19.12), and this and any paint on the wheels can be removed by using a paint remover such as Nitromors, carefully following the instructions and washing it off immediately if you get in on your skin – rubber gloves are essential for this operation.

When all is removed you can inspect the wheel for damage. Minor chipping from kerbing may be acceptable, and if very minor can be polished out, but anything significant will need a specialist repair, supposing this is possible, or a replacement.

The process of polishing or buffing is carried out by the application of polishing compounds that are slightly abrasive, each subsequent stage using a finer grade of abrasive. The first rule of the professional metal finisher is that the shape of the object must be preserved; it is all too easy, especially in the early stages of the process, to overdo things and unconsciously rub away corners or ridges or finish up with a concave rather than a flat surface.

This needs guarding against in the preparatory stages when any roughness such as pitting or minor damage is dealt with using, as appropriate, files, emery cloth or an abrasive wheel in the electric drill. Polishing is essentially a finishing operation and will not deal with major surface irregularities, and the surface must be smooth before the actual polishing procedure begins.

Polishing compounds and wheels (mops) are now much more easily available to the amateur than formerly, and they can be bought from mail order specialists or some tool shops. There are different grades of compound (known by metal finishers as soap, perhaps because of the shape of the commercially-used bars that look like old fashioned bar soap). Each grade has its own colour and is used for different metals and plastics, and there are different types and sizes of mops, which are made of varying types of cloth.

Once the wheels are free from surface damage and the metal is smooth there are two stages in polishing them. The first requires a stitched mop of suitable size in the electric drill or flexible shaft and the use of a compound known as Tripoli, which is brown in colour. The polish is pressed lightly and frequently to the rotating mop's periphery, which in turn is applied to the wheel, or

sections of it, to be polished. A light touch and slow movement of the mop across the surface is required and the mop should work away from edges rather than into them. If the polish builds up on the surface it can be polished out or later removed with white spirit.

When this is completed, wipe over the polished surface to remove any remaining Tripoli compound, and with a loosefold (unstitched) finishing mop loaded with green-coloured compound (Sovereign) repeat the polishing operation. At the end of this procedure the alloy should be bright and highly polished and any excess compound should be removed by careful wiping.

If the wheels are partially painted the non-painted areas and tyres should be masked off to protect the newly polished surfaces. Incidentally, masking tyres is always something of a bore and it is much easier to smear grease onto the side walls – paint will not adhere to it and it can be easily wiped off after spraying. Paint can be sprayed or brushed onto the appropriate areas, which

in some cases, as on the Dunlop wheels used on the Triumph Stag, were left rough-cast and not fettled or smoothed so that there will be a contrast between the polished and painted surfaces not only in colour but also in texture. When thoroughly dry, the wheels should be finished with one or two coats of transparent lacquer to preserve the shine on the alloy.

While you are at it you may as well give some attention to the wheel securing nuts, which will be either chromed or chemically treated to give a black finish. If they will not clean up with soap and water, or in the case of plated ones with a cleaning compound such as Solvol Autosol, you will have to have them refinished, or, which may be cheaper, replace them. Stainless steel ones are available for some cars.

Keep your polishes, and particularly the mops, separate otherwise those used for fine polishing will become contaminated with the coarser abrasive and cause scratches in the final finish, and do wear protective clothing and goggles as metal polishing is a dirty job.

Fig. 19.12. Lacquer lifting from an alloy wheel.

Appendix 1

Liquid petroleum gas

Liquid petroleum gas (LPG) has been used for a number of years and, especially in Europe, is available from many petrol filling stations; it is becoming increasingly available in the UK. Its use is actively encouraged by government as its toxic emissions are so much lower than those from petrol engines (about 0.25% compared to 2.5%) and tax concessions make it about half the price of petrol. This means, in effect, that cars with large engines, such as Aston Martins, Bentleys, Jaguars, Range Rovers, Rolls-Royces and most American cars

with a consumption of about 15mpg, will, if fitted with an LPG conversion, in terms of price, return the equivalent of about 30mpg. This at once removes one of the main objections that the buyer/restorer may have and opens up a much wider range of cars for the enthusiast.

LPG conversions are designed for three types of engine, the traditional carburettor variety, the later carburettor systems with microprocessor control for catalyser exhaust systems, and multi-point systems for injected engines.

In the UK, prices for the equipment in 2003 are in the region of £450, £650 and £850 respectively. Fitting is extra, but there is nothing that average restorers cannot do for themselves.

The kit contains all the parts necessary to make the conversion – Fig. A1 shows the multi-point kit. The main components, shown in Fig. A2 are the tank, ECU, fuel rail with injectors and a vaporizer (pressure reducer). Tanks come in different shapes and sizes depending on where you want to install it. The one shown is torroidal (doughnut) and fits in the spare wheel well.

Fig. A1. The complete kit for multi-point LPG conversion.

The liquid in the tank is piped via a solenoid-operated valve to the vaporizer which is heated by being tapped in to the heater hose, and then as gas to the fuel rail. The injectors, controlled by the ECU, feed nozzles in the manifold placed close to those for the petrol injectors. It is not necessary to remove the manifolds as they can be drilled and tapped in situ if a slow speed is used and the drill (and tap) greased to pick up any particles of metal not ejected by the tool.

The system is controlled by a switch (which also indicates the amount of liquid in the tank) and either petrol or gas can be instantly selected, though starting is always on petrol, the changeover to gas being automatic once the appropriate temperature has been reached.

On the simplest carburettor systems mixture adjustment is by simple adjustment of the vaporizer and can be set by means of a CO_2 meter (try your local MoT station) but ECU-equipped systems have to be set up by means of a computer system, the software for which is expensive and may not be worth buying for only one installation.

There are also a good many electrical connections to be made on the more sophisticated systems. If you are not confident about this it may pay you to do a deal with the kit supplier, whereby you undertake the mechanical installation and they do the electrical work and set up the system for you.

Gas is not quite as efficient as petrol so you may lose about 10%-15% of maximum speed, and a similar loss in terms of consumption as well as boot space

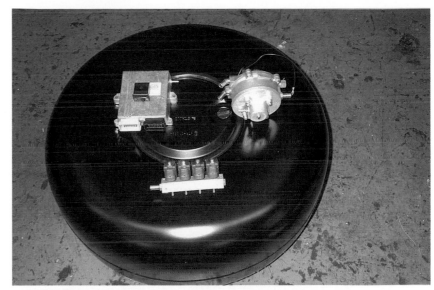

Fig. A2. The most important units – storage tank (pressure tested and marked), dedicated ECU and switch, water heated vaporizer and fuel rail with injectors.

Fig. A3. Setting up the system. One of the PC displays.

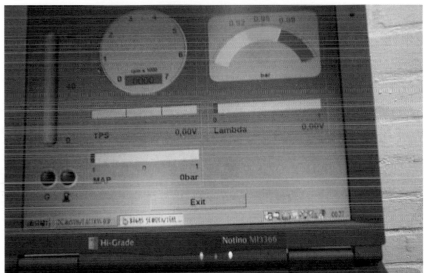

for the tank. To offset this LPG is cleaner both in the engine (oil changes need not be as frequent) and especially in the atmosphere, and very much cheaper, perhaps making your Limo or V8 monster into a daily driver rather than a weekend special?

This is what can be achieved – a beautifully restored Triumph TR3A. (John Colley)

Appendix 2

Useful information

SPECIALIST SUPPLIERS

Burlen Fuel Systems
Spitfire House, Castle Road,
Salisbury, Wiltshire,
England SP1 3SA
Tel. 01722 412500
Fax 01722 334221
www.burlen.co.uk
*SU carburettors and fuel pumps;
spares or complete units and fuel
system components for a very
wide range of vehicles. Zenith and
Stromberg CD carburettors.
Rebuilding of your own units. A
large and informative catalogue
available.*

Demon Tweeks Motorsport Direct
75 Ash Road South, Wrexham
Industrial Estate, Wrexham, North
Wales
Tel. 01978 664466
Fax 01978 664467
www.demon-tweeks.co.uk
*Very comprehensive catalogue of
chiefly motorsport related items –
fascinating reading on its own but
offering an amazing selection of
parts, accessories, tools,
equipment and clothing. Mainly
for enhancing the performance
and looks of cars, but many useful
replacement items also.*

**Frost Auto Restoration
Techniques Ltd**
Crawford Street, Rochdale,
Lancashire OL16 5NU
Tel. 01706 658619
Fax 01706 860338
www.frost.co.uk
*Catalogue of useful items for the
restorer; special paints, metal
polishing requisites, small tools,
repair kits for glass, trim and
upholstery, etc.*

Holden Vintage and Classic Ltd
Linton Trading Estate, Bromyard,
Herefordshire, HR7 4QT
Tel. 01885 488488
Fax 01855 488889
www.holden.co.uk
*Large catalogue of lamps,
electrical accessories, control
box/regulators, distributors,
switches, gasket materials, tools,
equipment and accessories
specifically for the classic and
vintage car.*

HPI
Dolphin House, PO Box 61, New
Street, Salisbury, Wilts SP1 2TB
Tel. 01722 422 422
www.hpicheck.com
*Hire Purchase Investigation. Check
whether the car you propose to
buy has outstanding HP, or
whether it is stolen or recovered.*

CSM Just Abrasives
Unit 2 Northern Road, Newark,
Nottinghamshire, NG24 2EH
Tel. 01636 688888
Fax 01636 688889
www.csmjustabrasives.co.uk
*Mail order abrasives/polishing
specialists*

MAGAZINES

There are numerous magazines
dealing with Classic cars. The more
general ones usually have articles
relating to restoration. They give
information on weak points of
specific models to help the buyer,
and typical prices of some
replaceable items, as well as values
of cars in various conditions.

In alphabetical order:
Car Mechanics (Kelsey Publishing Ltd)
Cars and Car Conversions (Link
House Magazines Ltd)
Classic & Sportscar (Haymarket
Publications Ltd)
Classic Car Mart (Trinity
Publications Ltd)
Thoroughbred and Classic Cars
(EMAP Active Ltd)
Classics (SPL)
Practical Classics and Car Restorer
(EMAP Active Ltd)
Old Bike Mart (Morton's
Motorcycle Media)
*Although this is devoted to
motorcycles there are many display
advertisements offering services
equally useful to car restorers.*
OBM Horncastle, Lincs LN9 6BR.
Available by subscription only: Tel.
01507 525772.

REFERENCE BOOKS
AND MANUALS

As mentioned in the text, there is
no substitute for a maker's
workshop manual, or the
appropriate Haynes Manual, to
give specific detail. Some one-
make clubs reproduce copies of
technical articles on particular
procedures or components.

Of more general interest are the
following:
Automotive Electrical Manual
(Haynes Publishing)
Fault Diagnosis (Lucas Technical
Series)
*How to Restore Wooden Body
Framing* (Osprey)
SU Workshop Manual (Burlen Fuel
Systems)
Automotive Carburettor Manual
(Haynes Publishing)
Zenith and CD Catalogue (Burlen
Fuel Systems).

Conversion factors

Imperial	Metric	Imperial
LENGTH (DISTANCE)		
Inches (in)	x 25.4 = Millimetres (mm)	x 0.0394 = Inches (in)
Feet (ft)	x 0.305 = Metres (m)	x 3.281 = Feet (ft)
Miles	x 1.609 = Kilometres (km)	x 0.621 = Miles
VOLUME (CAPACITY)		
Cubic inches (cu in; in3)	x 16.387 = Cubic centimetres (cc; cm3)	x 0.061 = Cubic inches (cu in; in3)
Imperial pints (Imp pt)	x 0.568 = Litres (l)	x 1.76 = Imperial pints (Imp pt)
Imperial gallons (Imp gal)	x 4.546 = Litres (l)	x 0.22 = Imperial gallons (0.833)
US gallons (US gal)	x 3.785 = Litres (l)	x 0.264 = US gallons (US gal)
MASS (WEIGHT)		
Pounds (lb)	x 0.454 = Kilograms (kg)	x 2.205 = Pounds (lb)
Hundredweight (cwt)	x 50.802 = Kilograms (kg)	x 0.020 = Hundredweight (cwt)
TORQUE		
Pounds-force feet (lbf ft; lb ft)	x 1.356 = Newton metres (Nm)	x 0.738 = Pounds-force feet (lbf ft; lb ft)
Pounds-force feet (lbf ft; lb ft)	x 0.138 = Kilograms-force metres (kgf m; km m)	x 7.233 = Pounds-force feet (lbf ft; lb ft)
POWER		
Horsepower (hp)	x 745.7 = Watts (W)	x 0.0013 = Horsepower (hp)
SPEED		
Miles per hour (miles/hr; mph)	x 1.609 = Kilometres per hour (km/hr; kph)	x 0.621 = Miles per hour (miles/hr; mph)
FUEL CONSUMPTION		
Miles per gallon (mpg)	x 0.354 = Kilometres per litre (km/l)	x 2.825 = Miles per gallon (mpg)

Index

other books from Haynes Publishing

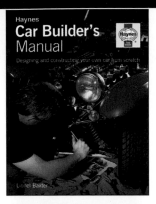

Car Builder's Manual
by Lionel Baxter
ISBN 1 85960 646 6

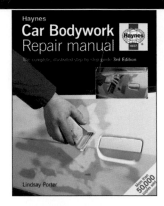

Car Bodywork Repair Manual (3rd Edition)
by Lindsay Porter
ISBN 1 85960 657 1

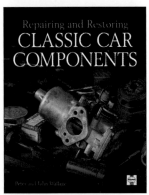

Repairing and Restoring Classic Car Components
by Peter and John Wallage
ISBN 1 85960 694 6

The Kit Car Manual
by Iain Ayre
ISBN 1 85960 962 7

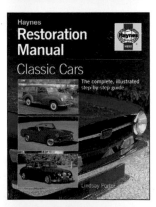

Classic Cars Restoration Manual
by Linday Porter
ISBN 1 85010 890 0

Build Your Own Sports Car for as little as £250 – and race it! (2nd Edition)
by Ron Champion
ISBN 1 85960 636 9

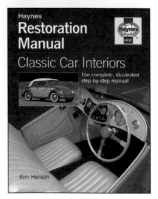

Classic Car Interiors Restoration Manual
by Kim Henson
ISBN 1 85010 932 X

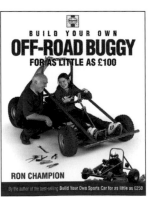

Build Your Own Off-Road Buggy for as little as £100
by Ron Champion
ISBN 1 85960 642 3